The Woman's Day Book
of GRANNY SQUARES
and other Carry-Along Crochet

 SIMON AND SCHUSTER ■ NEW YORK

PHOTO CREDITS

Jane Arnold   Pages 36, 40

Neal Barr   Page 54

Frances McLaughlin Gill   Pages 20, 32, 53, 62, 73, 82

Carmen Schiavone   Pages 12, 16, 30, 44, 46, 50, 58, 66, 68, 77, 88, 92, 96, 100, 103

Woman's Day Studio   Pages 60, 91, 105, 126, 148; detail photos, pages 12, 16, 58, 66, 68, 88, 92, 96, 100, 103, 135, 136, 148

Designed by Beri Greenwald
Manufactured in the United States of America

1   2   3   4   5   6   7   8   9   10

Library of Congress Cataloging in Publication Data

The Woman's day book of granny squares and other
* carry-along crochet.*
* 1. Crocheting.*
TT825.W63   746.4'34   74-32183
ISBN 0-671-21961-8

CONTENTS

INTRODUCTION

In its more than 37 years of publication *Woman's Day*, always in the forefront of the needlework field, has singled out the "granny square" as a surefire winner. And rightly so. Small wonder, then, that for decades its many creative designers have produced an endless stream of ideas. Literally hundreds of exciting new projects incorporating granny squares have graced *Woman's Day*'s pages—and always to the delight of its readers. This book represents the best of the best — dozens of granny designs, carefully selected for their timeless charm, versatility, and practical stylishness for today's living.

Making colorful afghans and bedspreads and blankets by joining small squares of the same size is one of the most traditional and American forms of crochet. In fact, in parts of Europe it is called American crochet. But on this side of the Atlantic it's been known as granny crochet for as long as anyone can remember. It springs up in popularity with each new generation and is as popular today as it was when your great-grandmother did it, and for the very same reason — it's portable. You can keep small amounts of yarn tucked in your purse and whip up a few units between bus stops or at the hairdresser's. Just shake out the sand, and the squares you make at the beach will be the same as the ones you made in front of TV.

Another major attraction of the granny square is that it's piecemeal work, convenient to start and stop. Unlike more complex crochet, it seldom requires you to refer to the written directions — you always know where you are in the pattern. Moreover it's economical — leftover yarns can be put to good use in a collection of multicolor squares. Even the tiniest scrap will make the first round of a square. The wildest colors combine beautifully in the mad jumble of a traditional granny afghan. And unrelated types of yarn can be used successfully — for example, mohair with knitting worsted, tweed with sports yarn. Even yarns of varying weights can be used in the same square.

And although the work is repetitive enough to keep your hands happily occupied while you're thinking about — or watching — something else, the variety of granny squares that can be made from innumerable yarn and color combinations prevents a granny square project from turning into a bore. And granny squares give you ample scope for real creativity. A pile of squares is like the elements of a collage. Squares can be shuffled and manipulated until the arrangement satisfies your most demanding sense of design and color.

One of the great things about granny crochet is its versatility. Once you have begun working with grannies you will find endless ways to use them in everything from bedspreads to bikinis. Glance through the following pages and you will find dozens of projects just waiting for you to pick up yarn and crochet hook. If you are an experienced crocheter, there's no reason why you can't begin a design in the next five minutes — providing you have the right yarn and hook. You can leave the technical information in the last part of this book for later reference.

If you are a beginning crocheter, perhaps you had better browse through the following pages for inspiration, then turn to page 109 to pick up some of the tips and information that will turn you into a granny square expert. In no time at all you will be able to tackle even the most elaborate project. One article may require 10 grannies, another 180 — but the afghan is no more difficult than the little cap.

The Woman's Day Book
of GRANNY SQUARES
and other Carry-Along Crochet

The Projects

OUT-OF-THE-BLUE JACKET

This is a real find — a wear-over-everything cardigan jacket. This treasure can top pants and skirts and would look great over a simple lightweight dress. If you are not the blue type, try deep burgundy for the main color; gray or beige would make the jacket even more versatile.

Although this is an ambitious project requiring 68 grannies, it's really not much more difficult than a simple scarf. A granny is a granny. Triangular grannies give shape to the neck and shoulders. The graceful shaping over hips and at underarms is achieved through gussets.

Size One size fits 12 to 16.

Materials Knitting worsted, 17 ounces royal blue for main color, 1 ounce each gold, beige, medium blue, light blue, aqua, dark rose, Kelly green, dark green, lavender, purple, pale peach, light pink, turquoise, orange, moss green and bright pink; steel crochet hook No. 00 *or the size that will give you the correct gauge;* tapestry needle.

Gauge Each square measures 4¼".

Squares (make 48 for jacket and 10 for each sleeve.) Starting at center, ch 6, join with sl st to form ring.

1st rnd Ch 3, work 2 dc in ring, (ch 1, 3-dc shell in ring) 3 times; ch 1; join with sl st to top of ch-3. Break off.

2nd rnd Sl st in any ch-1 sp, ch 3, in same sp work 2 dc, ch 1 and 3 dc (first corner), * ch 1, in next ch-1 sp work 3 dc, ch 1 and 3 dc (another corner). Repeat from * twice more; ch 1; join. Break off.

3rd rnd Sl st in any ch-1 corner sp and work a first corner in same sp, * ch 1, 3-dc shell in next ch-1 sp, ch 1, work corner in next corner sp. Repeat from * twice more; ch 1, shell in next sp, ch 1; join. Break off.

4th rnd Sl st in any ch-1 corner sp and work a first corner in same sp, * (ch 1, shell in next ch-1 sp) twice; ch 1, work corner in next corner sp. Repeat from * twice more; (ch 1, shell in next sp) twice; ch 1; join. Break off.

5th rnd Sl st in any ch-1 corner sp and work a first corner in same sp, * ch 1, work shell in next ch-1 sp. Repeat from * to next corner, ch 1, work a corner in next corner sp. Continue around in pattern; join. Break off. Work first 4 rnds of each square in assorted colors and 5th rnd always in main color.

Triangles (make 6) 1st row Starting at center of one edge, ch 5; in 5th ch from hook work 3 dc, ch 1, 3 dc, ch 1 and 1 dc. Break off.

2nd row Sl st in first ch-4 lp, ch 4, work 3 dc in same lp, ch 1, in next ch-1 sp work 3 dc, ch 1 and 3 dc (corner), ch 1, in last sp work 3 dc, ch 1 and 1 dc. Break off.

3rd row Sl st in first ch-4 lp, ch 4, 3 dc in same lp, ch 1, 3 dc in next ch-1 sp, ch 1, corner in next ch-1 corner sp, ch 1, 3 dc in next sp, ch 1, in last sp work 3 dc, ch 1 and 1 dc. Break off.

4th row Sl st in first ch-4 lp, ch 4, 3 dc in same lp, (ch 1, 3 dc in next ch-1 sp) twice; ch 1, corner in ch-1 corner sp, (ch 1, 3 dc in next sp) twice; ch 1, in last sp work 3 dc, ch 1 and 1 dc. Break off.

5th row Sl st in first ch-4 lp, ch 4, 3 dc in same lp, * ch 1, 3 dc in next sp. Repeat from * to corner, ch 1, work corner in corner sp, ** ch 1, 3 dc in next sp. Repeat from ** to last sp, in last sp work 3 dc, ch 1 and 1 dc. Break off. Work first 4 rows in assorted colors and 5th row in main color.

To Assemble: Body Arrange and pin 48 squares and 2 triangles, wrong side up, according to Diagram 1. Whipstitch together on wrong side with main color and tapestry needle, but do not sew the 4 seams marked from X to Y. Try on jacket. If you need more "give" around the hip section of jacket, remove pins from the 4 seams and work narrow gussets on the right side as follows: Attach main color at an X, work sc along edges of the 2 squares to Y. Break off. Repeat along the adjoining 2 squares. Now whipstitch the seam. Repeat process along remaining 3 pinned seams. Sew shoulder seams.

Sleeves Join 10 squares and 2 triangles as for body, following Diagram 2. **To Shape Underarm Gusset** With right side facing you, attach main color to corner sp at Z on Diagram 2. **1st row** Ch 3, work 2 dc in same sp, (ch 1, 3 dc in next sp) 12 times; sl st in each of next 3 dc and in next sp; ch 1, turn. **2nd row** Sl st in each of next 7 sts, ch 2, work 2 dc in next sp, (ch 1, 3 dc in next sp) 11 times; ch 4, turn. **3rd row** Sk first 3 dc, work 3 dc in next sp, (ch 1, 3 dc in next sp) 3 times; sl st in next 32 sts; ch 1, turn. **4th row** Sl st in next 38 sts, ch 2, 2 dc in next sp, (ch 1, 3 dc in next sp) twice. Break off. With wrong side facing you, work underarm gusset along opposite side of sleeve; whipstitch sleeve seam.

Cuffs Attach main color in a corner sp next to seam on lower edge of sleeve. **1st rnd** Ch 3, work 2 dc in corner sp, * ch 1, 3 dc in next sp. Repeat from * around sleeve edge, ch 1; join. **2nd rnd** Ch 4, * 3 dc in next sp, ch 1. Repeat from * around, ending with 2 dc in last sp; sl st in 3rd ch of ch-4. Repeat last 2 rnds until cuff measures about 5". Break off. Fold back cuff.

Work other sleeve in same manner. Whipstitch sleeves to jacket, centering top square at shoulder seam.

Jacket Edging With right side facing you, attach main color to corner sp at left front neck edge (dot on Diagram 1) and work completely around jacket edge as follows: **1st rnd** Ch 3, work 2 dc in corner sp, * ch 1, 3 dc in next sp. Repeat from * around, working in seam joinings as well as in sps, and working 3 dc, ch 1 and 3 dc at lower front corners; ch 1; join. **2nd rnd** Sl st in each of next 2 dc and in next sp, ch 3, work 2 dc in same sp, * ch 1, 3 dc in next sp. Repeat from * along left front, lower edge and right front, working corners in corner sps at lower front corners and ending in right front neck edge corner, ** ch 1, 3 sc in next sp. Repeat from ** along triangle, back neck and other triangle; ch 1; join. Break off.

Ties: Bobbles (make 6) With main color, ch 6. Join with sl st to form ring. **1st rnd** Ch 3, work 10 dc in ring; join with sl st to top of ch-3. **2nd rnd** Ch 3, dc in each dc around; join. **3rd rnd** Ch 3, * holding back on hook the last lp of each dc, work dc in each of next 5 dc, y o, draw through all 6 lps on hook. Repeat from * once more. Break off.

Cords With main color double, crochet a chain 23" long. Break off. Sew a bobble to each end. Make 2 more ties. Following photograph for placement, insert bobbles of ties through spaces on front squares.

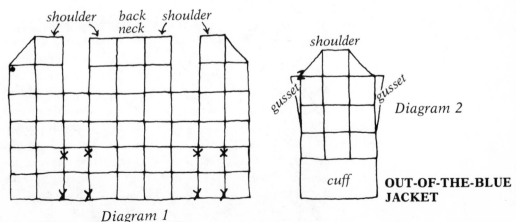

shoulder *back neck* *shoulder*

Diagram 1

shoulder

gusset *gusset*

Diagram 2

cuff

OUT-OF-THE-BLUE JACKET

VICTORIAN VEST

This romantic vest goes over a tailored shirt with the same ease it once might have complemented a late-nineties shirtwaist. The basic design of the front is an ornate granny with a weblike center. The spectacular back is a simple lacy granny composed of shells and a network of chains. Although it looks difficult, it isn't. Amazingly, all it requires is two stitches—chain and double crochet.

Sizes Small (6-8) [medium (10-12)]. Vest measures 15″ [17″] across from underarm to underarm when stretched slightly.

Materials Brunswick Pomfret sport yarn, 2 (2-ounce) skeins rose No. 572 (color A), 1 skein pink No. 515 (B); steel crochet hook No. 1 [0 for medium] *or the size that will give you the correct gauge;* tapestry needle.

NOTE: Vest is composed of 3 types of squares. The small ones for front and a variation for straps are shown in the photograph. The large one for the back is not shown.

Front Squares (make 8) Each square measures 4″ [4½″].

With A, starting at center, ch 6. Join with sl st to form ring.

1st rnd Ch 8, (work tr in ring, ch 4) 7 times; sl st in 4th ch of ch-8 (8 spokes).

2nd rnd Work 6 sc in each sp around.

3rd rnd Sc in next sc, (h dc in next sc, dc in next 8 sc, h dc in next sc, sc in each of next 2 sc) 4 times, ending last repeat with 1 sc instead of 2 (4 petals made with 12 sts each).

4th rnd Sl st in next 6 sts, ch 8, sc in same st as last sl st, ch 5, sk next 3 sts, sc in next st, ch 5, sk next 4 sts, sc in next st, ch 5, sk next 2 sts, dc in next st, * ch 5, sc in same st, ch 5, sk 3 sts, sc in next st, ch 5, sk next 4 sts, sc in next st, ch 5, sk next 2 sts, dc in next st. Repeat from * twice more, ending last repeat by joining with sl st in 3rd ch of ch-8 instead of dc in next st.

5th rnd * Work 11 sc in next ch-5 corner lp (ch 5, sc in next sp) 3 times; ch 5. Repeat from * 3 times more; join with sl st in first sc.

6th rnd Ch 4, tr in each of next 10 sc, * sc in next sp, (ch 5, sc in next sp) 3 times; tr in next 11 sc. Repeat from * twice more; sc in next sp, (ch 5, sc in next sp) 3 times; join with sl st in top of ch-4. Break off.

Strap Squares (make 6) Each square measures 3½" [4"].

Using B, work as for Front Square through 3rd rnd; join with sl st in next st. Break off. Use A for 4th, 5th and 6th rnds.

4th rnd Sl st in 6th st (4th dc) on any petal. Repeat 4th rnd of Front Square from ch-8.

5th rnd * Work 11 sc in next corner ch-5 lp (corner), sc in next sp, (ch 5, sc in next sp) twice. Repeat from * 3 times more; join.

6th rnd * Work sc in each sc around corner, sc in each sc and in each ch st across next 2 sps. Repeat from * 3 times more; join. Break off.

Back Square (make 1)—Square measures 12½" [13½"].

Using B, work as for Front Square through 5th rnd.

6th rnd Ch 4, tr in next 10 sc (corner fan), * (ch 5, sc in next sp) 4 times; ch 5, tr in next 11 sc (another corner fan). Repeat from * twice more: (ch 5, sc in next sp) 4 times; ch 5; join with sl st to top of ch-4.

7th rnd Ch 5, sk next 4 tr, dc in next tr, ch 5, sc in same tr (corner lp), ch 5, * sc in next ch-5 sp, ch 5 * . Repeat from * to * to next corner fan, sk next 5 tr, dc in next tr, ch 5, sc in same tr, ch 5. Repeat from * to * to next corner fan. Continue around in pattern, ending with sc at base of first ch-5. Break off.

8th rnd Work 11 sc in any corner lp, ch 5, * sc in next sp, ch 5 *. Repeat from * to * to next corner lp, 11 sc in corner lp, ch 5. Repeat from * to * to next corner lp. Continue around in pattern, ending by joining with sl st in first sc.

9th rnd Ch 4, tr in next 10 sc (fan), ch 5, * sc in next sp, ch 5 *. Repeat from * to * to next sc corner group, tr in next 11 sc (fan), ch 5. Repeat from * to * to next corner group. Continue around in pattern, ending by joining with sl st in top of ch-4.

Repeat 7th, 8th and 9th rnds twice more. Break off. Work with A for 16th rnd through 19th rnd, repeating 7th, 8th, 9th and 7th rnds. Break off.

To Assemble See assembly diagram. Hold two Front Squares together (1 on diagram) wrong sides facing. With matching yarn and tapestry needle, whipstitch squares together along one side. Join 2 groups of 4 squares each for fronts as shown on diagram. Then join 2 strips of 3 Strap Squares each for straps (2 on diagram). Join a front to one end of each strap, then join the large square to opposite ends of straps for back. Whipstitch side edges between dots on back square.

Front Edging With right side facing you, with B work 1 row sc along front edges, starting in first tr of fan at lower corner and ending in last tr of fan at top corner. Break off.

Tie Work with double strand of B. Crochet a chain long enough to lace through holes of squares along front and tie in bow at waist. Sc in 2nd ch from hook and in each ch across. Break off.

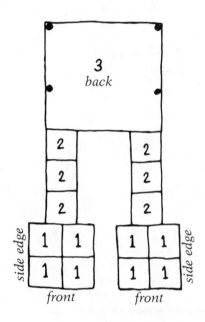

PATCHWORK PULLOVER

PATCHWORK PULLOVER

Just like a collage of granny squares, big and little, is this wearable pullover made of knitting worsted. The finished squares are pinned to a piece of scrap fabric and the blank spaces are filled in with bits of single crochet – almost like filling in the spaces in a jigsaw puzzle.

Size Sweater fits sizes 8 through 14 and measures about 18" across front at underarms. Adjustments can be made with side gussets and a wider border for sizes 16 and 18.

Materials Coats & Clark's wool knitting worsted, 8 ounces wine rose No. 760, 1 ounce each blue jewel No. 818, amethyst No. 588, taupe No. 356, lilac No. 586, Paddy green No. 686, Mexicana (ombré) No. 950, scarlet No. 909, light Oxford No. 403, navy No. 858, tangerine No. 253, baby yellow No. 224, dark gold No. 602, dark turquoise No. 515, wood brown No. 360 (see **Yarns** below); aluminum crochet hook size G *or the size that will give you the correct gauge;* scrap fabric about 20" square.

Yarns Some of the colors specified can be purchased only in 4-ounce skeins. If you wish to substitute other colors or use any yarns of knitting worsted weight you might have on hand, the exact amount of yarn used in each color has been indicated.

Gauge 4-rnd square=4¼"; 4 sc=1"; 4 sc rows=1".

NOTE: The arrangement of the squares has been changed slightly from the original for a better fitting garment.

Squares Starting at center, ch 4. Join with sl st to form ring.

1st rnd Ch 3, work 2 dc in ring, (ch 1, 3-dc shell in ring) 3 times; ch 1; join with sl st to top of ch-3. Break off.

2nd rnd Sl st in any ch-1 sp, ch 3, in same sp work 2 dc, ch 1 and 3 dc (first corner), * ch 1, in next ch-1 sp work 3 dc, ch 1 and 3 dc (another corner). Repeat from * twice more; ch 1; join. Break off.

3rd rnd Sl st in any ch-1 corner sp and work a first corner in same sp, * ch 1, 3-dc shell in next ch-1 sp, ch 1, work corner in next corner sp. Repeat from * twice more; ch 1, shell in next sp, ch 1; join. Break off.

4th rnd Sl st in any ch-1 corner sp and work a first corner in same sp, * (ch 1, shell in next ch-1 sp) twice; ch 1, work corner in next corner sp. Repeat from * twice more; (ch 1, shell in next sp) twice; ch 1; join. Break off.

5th rnd Sl st in any ch-1 corner sp and work a first corner in same sp, * ch 1, work shell in next ch-1 sp. Repeat from * to next corner, ch 1, work a corner in next corner sp. Continue around in pattern; join. Break off.

Work each rnd in a different color. The colors and number of rnds for each square are as follows:

Front: Square 1 Blue, amethyst, taupe, lilac. **Square 2** Wine, green. **Square 3** 2 rnds Mexicana. **Square 4** Lilac, wine, scarlet. **Square 5** Scarlet, wine, light Oxford, navy, taupe. **Square 6** Taupe, blue. **Square 7** Taupe, wine. **Square 8** Green, light Oxford, taupe, tangerine, navy. **Square 9** Blue, yellow, gold. **Square 10** Tangerine, gold, navy, turquoise. **Square 11** Brown, amethyst, taupe. **Square 12** Scarlet, green, lilac, gold. **Square 13** Taupe, blue, green, brown, wine. **Square 14** Yellow, scarlet, amethyst. **Square 15** Navy, turquoise. **Square 16** Yellow, scarlet, brown. **Square 17** Lilac, Mexicana, scarlet, Mexicana. **Square 18** Wine, light Oxford, lilac. **Square 19** Gold, taupe, scarlet.

Patchwork On fabric, draw 16" x 19" rectangle. Following diagram, pin squares to fabric. Work shaded areas on diagram in stripes of desired colors as follows:

1st row Starting in a corner, work sc evenly along edge of a square; ch 1, turn. **2nd row** Sc in each sc across; ch 1, turn. Work even until piece fits shaded area. Break off. (NOTE: If desired work each row in a different color.) In this manner fill all shaded areas on diagram and any additional areas necessary to complete patchwork. Pin or baste all pieces together to form rectangle that will hold together when removed from fabric. Remove pins from fabric and whipstitch pieces together.

Border With right side facing you, attach scarlet with sl st in corner sp at X on diagram. **1st rnd** Work dc across upper and lower edges, sc across side edges, 2 dc and 1 sc in each corner sp; join with sl st to first st. Break off. Working 1 sc in each st around and 3 sc in center st of each corner, work 1 rnd each amethyst and lilac and 2 rnds wine. Piece should measure about 18" across. For a wider sweater, work additional rows of sc along sides; or, if you need width at hipline only, gussets can be added later.

Back Work same as for front.

With right sides facing, leaving center 9″ open at top edge for neck, pin shoulders together and whipstitch.

Sleeves With right side facing you, place underarm markers on side edges of front and back, 8″ down from shoulder seams. Attach wine at left front marker. **1st row** Work 60 sc evenly along armhole edge to left back marker; ch 1, turn. **2nd row** Sc in each sc across; ch 1, turn. **3rd (dec) row** Draw up lp in each of first 2 sc, y o and draw through all 3 lps on hook (1 sc dec), sc in each sc across to within last 2 sc, dec 1 sc; ch 1, turn. (Work even for 2 rows; repeat dec row) 3 times (52 sc). Work even until sleeve measures 8½″. Work 2 rows each scarlet, yellow, gold, brown, blue, green and lilac, decreasing 1 st at beg and end of first row of each color stripe (38 sc). With wine, dec as before at beg and end of every other row twice (34 sc). With wine, work even until sleeve measures 16″, or 1″ less than desired length. With brown, work 3 rows even, then work dec row. Break off.

Attach wine at right back marker and work right sleeve in same manner as left. Whipstitch sleeve seams. Pin side seams; try on sweater.

For graduated width along hipline (if necessary), make 2 gussets as follows:

Gussets (optional) Starting at upper point of gusset with wine, ch 2. **1st row** Work 2 sc in 2nd ch from hook; ch 1, turn. **2nd row** Work 2 sc in each sc (4 sc); ch 1, turn. **3rd and 4th rows** Sc in each sc across; ch 1, turn. **5th (inc) row** Sc in each sc across, working 2 sc in 3rd sc (1 sc inc); ch 1, turn. Work 2 rows even. Inc 1 sc in center of next row. Repeat last 3 rows until gusset is desired size. Break off. Matching lower edges, pin gusset between side edges of front and back; with wine, whipstitch gussets and complete side seams to armholes.

Finishing Attach blue at lower edge. **1st rnd** Work sc evenly around; join with sl st to first sc. Break off. Work 1 rnd each taupe, Mexicana and scarlet and 2 rnds brown. Break off.

BOLEROS FOR GIRLS–BIG AND LITTLE

A batch of small-size granny squares in white and two pretty colors produce the trimmest little boleros this side of a gypsy caravan. Triangles at front neckline and under arms add a neat dressmaker touch.

Big Girl's Bolero

Sizes Small [medium—large]. Garment width around under-arms, 32½" [37"—41"]; length is 15¼" [17¼"—17¼"].

Materials Fingering yarn, 6 [7—7] ounces of main color (A), 2 [2—4] ounces each of B and C; crochet hook size D *or the size that will give you the correct gauge;* hook and eye; tapestry needle.

Gauge Each square measures 2".

Squares **(make 39** [52—56]**)** of the following colors:
Ch and 1st rnd, B; **2nd rnd,** C; **3rd rnd,** A. Make 40 [52—58] reversing colors for **1st and 2nd rnds.**

Starting at center, ch 6. Join with sl st to form ring.

1st rnd Ch 3, work 2 dc in ring, (ch 2, 3-dc shell in ring) 3 times; ch 2; join with sl st to top of ch-3. Break off.

2nd rnd With new color, sl st in any ch-sp; ch 3, in same sp work 2 dc, ch 2 and 3 dc (first corner), * ch 2, in next sp work 3 dc, ch 2 and 3 dc (another corner). Repeat from * twice more, ch 2; join. Break off.

3rd rnd With color A, sl st in any corner sp and work a first corner in same sp, * ch 2, 3 dc in next ch-sp, ch 2, work another corner in next corner sp. Repeat from * twice more; ch 2, 3 dc in next ch-sp, ch 2; join. Break off.

Triangles Make 4 of the first color combination and 2 in the second combination used for squares. Starting at the center of one side, ch 6. Join with sl st in first ch to form ring.

1st row Ch 3, 3 dc in ring, ch 2, 4 dc in ring. Break off.

2nd row Sl st between ch and first dc of 1st row; ch 3, 3 dc in same sp, ch 2, in next sp work 3 dc, ch 2 and 3 dc (corner made), ch 2, 4 dc between last 2 sts. Break off.

3rd row Sl st between ch and first dc; ch 3, 3 dc in same sp, ch 2, 3 dc in next ch-sp, ch 2, work corner in corner sp, ch 2, 3 dc in next sp, ch 2, 4 dc between last 2 sts; sl st along base of triangle edge. Break off.

Finishing Hold 2 squares of opposite colors tog with right sides facing. With A, sc them tog along one side. Join to remaining pieces following diagram, being sure to alternate colors.

Right Front Shoulder With A and right side facing, insert hook in corner ch-sp at neck and draw up a lp, ch 1, 1 h dc in corner sp, (1 h dc in sp between next 2 dc) twice; 1 h dc in next ch-2

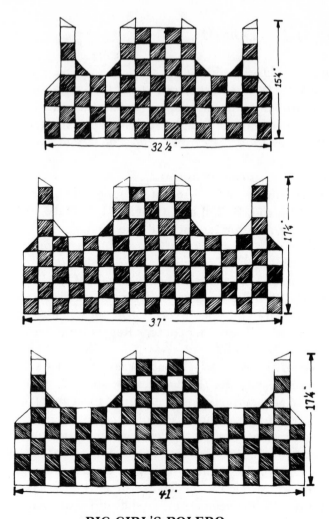

BIG GIRL'S BOLERO

sp; (1 h dc in sp between next 2 dc) twice; sl st in next ch-2 sp; turn. Sk sl st, sl st in each of next 3 h dc working through both lps of the h dc, 3 h dc. Break off.

Left Back Shoulder Work as for Right Front Shoulder.

Right Back and Left Front Shoulders With wrong side facing, work as for previous shoulders. Sew shoulder seams.

Border With A and right side facing, begin at lower edge of back and draw lp through. **1st rnd** Ch 1, work 1 h dc between each st (9 h dc across each square) and 4 h dc into each ch-sp at the corners of the bolero. Work through both lps of each sl st along edge of triangles. Join with sl st in starting ch.

2nd rnd Ch 1, h dc in each h dc of 1st rnd working 2 h dc into each corner sp. Increase 1 h dc at lower edge of triangle at neck and dec 1 st across upper part of triangle. Join with sl st in starting ch-1.

3rd rnd Sc from left to right around to form picot edge.

Armholes Work as for border; on 2nd rnd, dec 1 st at each underarm corner. Break off.

Sew hook and eye to front neck.

Little Girl's Bolero

Sizes 2 to 3 [6 to 8—10 to 12]. Garment width around underarms, 21¾″ [26″—30½″]; length, 10¾″ [13″—13″].

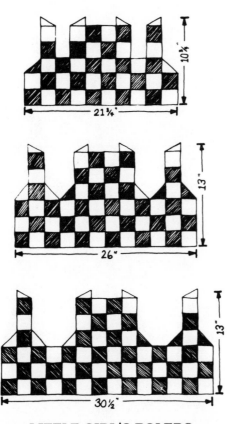

LITTLE GIRL'S BOLERO

Materials Fingering yarn, 4 ounces main color (A), 2 ounces each colors B and C; crochet hook size D *or the size that will give you the correct gauge;* hook and eye; tapestry needle.

Gauge Each square measures 2".

Squares Make 20 [27—30] in each of the following color combinations: **Ch and 1st rnd,** B; **2nd rnd,** C; **3rd rnd,** A. **Ch and 1st rnd,** C; **2nd rnd,** B; **3rd rnd,** A. Work same as squares for Big Girl's Bolero.

Triangles Make 1 [3—3] in each of the color combinations used for squares. Work same as triangles for Big Girl's Bolero.

Finishing Complete same as Big Girl's Bolero.

POP-OVER PONCHO

Crocheted in both worsted and mohair in shades of one color, this pop-over poncho is particularly comfortable. A shoulder zipper lets you put it on without disturbing even the fluffiest hairdo. Extra squares inserted diagonally in the outside rows produce a mini-ruffled border.

Size One size fits all. Poncho measures 32" from center front neck to lower point.

Materials Bear Brand knitting worsted, 1 (4-ounce) skein medium Oxford No. 70 (color A), 4 skeins dark Oxford No. 71 (B); Bucilla Supra Mohair, 10 balls (40 grams or about 1½ ounces each) dark gray No. 33 (C); aluminum crochet hook size E *or the size that will give you the correct gauge;* 18" separating-type zipper.

Gauge Each square measures 3".

Squares (make 155) Starting at center with A, ch 5. Join with sl st to form ring.

1st rnd Ch 3, work 2 dc in ring, (ch 2, 3 dc in ring) 3 times; ch 2; join with sl st to top of ch-3. Break off.

2nd rnd With B, sl st in any ch-2 sp, ch 3, in same sp work 2 dc, ch 1 and 3 dc (first corner) * ch 1, in next ch-2 sp work 3 dc, ch 1 and 3 dc (another corner). Repeat from * twice more; ch 1, join. Do not break off.

3rd rnd Sl st in each of next 2 dc and in ch-1 sp, work a first corner in same sp, * ch 1, 3 dc in next sp (shell made), ch 1, work corner in next corner sp. Repeat from * twice more; ch 1, shell in next sp, ch 1; join. Break off.

4th rnd With C, sl st in any corner sp and work a first corner in same sp, * (ch 1, shell in next ch-1 sp) twice; ch 1, work corner in next corner sp. Repeat from * twice more; (ch 1, shell in next sp) twice; ch 1, join. Break off.

Joining Holding 2 squares with wrong sides tog, with C, working through both pieces, sc along one edge (ridge will form on right side). Join 6 strips of 14 squares each in this manner to form rectangle.

Zipper Edge and Neck Shaping Make 2 strips of 6 squares each; join each to last strip joined on rectangle, leaving 2 center squares on rectangle free for neck edge. Fold piece in half

crosswise for poncho shape. Insert zipper along open shoulder and side.

Border Attach a square to each motif along lower edge of poncho, but do not join these squares to each other. Also put a square at front and back points. To produce the flouncy effect, join a square diagonally between 2 squares all along border. These additional squares will form points at lower edge.

CHILD'S PATCHWORK SWEATER

The unusual technique found in the Patchwork Pullover will work for almost anything you have in mind, from skirts to afghans. Here's a lively sweater for little girls made in the same way. Grannies of various sizes are pinned to a piece of scrap fabric and the blank spaces between are filled in with single crochet.

Size 4 through 6. Sweater measures 13½" across back at underarms and 13" from back of neck to lower edge. Adjustments can be made for slightly larger size by working wider borders around patchwork, or, for smaller size, by omitting side gussets.

Materials Bernat Berella Germantown acrylic yarn, 3 ounces China rose No. 7223, 2 ounces purple No. 7292, ½ ounce each jockey red No. 7234, caramel No. 7217, Shannon green No. 7289, orange No. 7254, flag blue (turquoise) No. 7263, lavender No. 7291, Roman gold No. 7207, walnut No. 7212, honey (yellow) No. 7203 and marine blue No. 7267 (see **Yarns** below); aluminum crochet hook size F *or the size that will give you the correct gauge;* scrap fabric about 13" square; tapestry needle.

Yarns The yarn specified can be purchased only in 2-ounce balls. If you wish to substitute other colors or use any yarns of knitting-worsted weight you might have on hand, the exact amount of yarn used in each color has been indicated.

Gauge 3-rnd square=3"; 9 sc=2"; 9 sc rows=2".

Squares Starting at center, ch 4 Join with sl st to form ring.

1st rnd Ch 3, work 2 dc in ring, (ch 1, 3-dc shell in ring) 3 times; ch 1; join with sl st to top of ch-3. Break off.

2nd rnd Sl st in any ch 1 sp, ch 3, in same sp work 2 dc, ch 1 and 3 dc (first corner), * ch 1, in next ch-1 sp work 3 dc, ch 1 and 3 dc (another corner). Repeat from * twice more; ch 1; join. Break off.

3rd rnd Sl st in any ch-1 corner sp and work a first corner in same sp, * ch 1, 3-dc shell in next ch-1 sp, ch 1, work corner in next corner sp. Repeat from * twice more; ch 1, shell in next sp. ch 1; join. Break off.

4th rnd Sl st in any ch-1 corner sp and work a first corner in same sp, * (ch 1, shell in next ch-1 sp) twice; ch 1, work corner in next corner sp. Repeat from * twice more; (ch 1, shell in next sp) twice; ch 1; join. Break off.

5th rnd Sl st in any ch-1 corner sp and work a first corner in same sp, * ch 1, work shell in next ch-1 sp. Repeat from * to next corner; ch 1, work a corner in next corner sp. Continue around in pattern; join. Break off.

Work each rnd in a different color. The colors and number of rnds for each square are as follows:

Front: Square 1 Orange, green, caramel, red. **Square 2** Flag blue, purple, lavender. **Square 3** Red, lavender, rose. **Square 4** Red, gold, walnut. **Square 5** Orange, flag blue, walnut. **Square 6** Rose, red. **Square 7** Marine blue, green. **Square 8** Marine blue, flag blue, honey, purple, caramel.

Patchwork On fabric, draw 11½"-wide x 10¾" rectangle. Following diagram for child's sweater, work same as for **Patchwork** in Patchwork Pullover, page 22.

Border With right side facing you, attach rose with sl st in corner sp at X on diagram. **1st rnd** Work sc evenly around patchwork, working 3 sc in each corner; join with sl st to first sc. Working 1 sc in each st around and 3 sc in center st of each corner, work 1 more rnd rose and 2 rnds purple. Piece should measure about 13½" across.

Back Work same as for front.

With right sides together, leaving center 7" open at top edge for neck, pin shoulders and whipstitch.

Sleeves With right side facing you, place underarm markers on side edges of front and back, 6" down from shoulder seams. Attach rose at left front marker. **1st row** Work 54 sc evenly along armhole edge to left back marker; ch 1, turn. **2nd row** Sc in each sc across; ch 1, turn. Work even until sleeve measures 4¾" from beg. Then work stripes of 2 rows each lavender, marine blue, flag blue, honey, red, walnut and purple and, at same time, when piece measures 6½" from beg, to dec 1 sc at beg and end of every other row 4 times. With purple, work even on 46 sc until sleeve measures 10" or desired length. Break off.

Attach rose at right back marker and work right sleeve in same manner as left.

Side Gussets (make 2) Starting at upper point of gusset with lavender, ch 2. **1st row** Work 2 dc in 2nd ch from hook; ch 3, turn. **2nd row** Work dc in first dc, 2 dc in 2nd dc (4 c, counting ch-3 as 1 dc); ch 3, turn. **3rd and 4th rows** Sk first dc, dc in each dc across; ch 3, turn. Do not ch 3 at end of 4th row. Break off.

Turn. **5th (inc) row** With red, sl st in first dc, ch 3, dc in same dc (inc made), sc in each dc to last dc, 2 dc in last dc (6 dc); ch 3, turn. Work 2 rows even. Break off. Repeat 5th row with walnut (8 dc). Work 2 rows even. Break off. Repeat 5th row with purple (10 dc). Work 2 rows even. Repeat 5th row (12 dc). Break off.

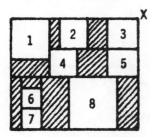

**CHILD'S
PATCHWORK SWEATER**

Matching lower edges, pin gussets between side edges of front and back. With purple, whipstitch gussets, remainder of side seams (if any) and sleeve seams.
Finishing: 1st rnd With purple, work sc in each st around lower edge, decreasing 4 sts evenly spaced; join with sl st in first sc. Repeat last rnd once more. Break off.

MILLEFLEURS SKIRT

For elegant evenings at home or in faraway places, work a palette of colors into a long, slim skirt. The squares grow larger from waist to border–three sizes of crochet hooks are the trick. Worked in a lightweight yarn, the skirt is sleek and flattering and is not too bulky to be packed in a small suitcase for a festive weekend in the country.

Sizes Misses' small [medium—large]. Garment width around hip, about 38½" [41¼"—44"]; waist measurement before insertion of elastic or ribbon, about 35" [37½"—40"]. Length as shown, 40" (omit lower rings for shorter skirt).

Materials Fingering yarn (3-ply), 6 ounces black (main color—MC), 1 ounce each light blue, medium blue, royal blue, mint, emerald, shocking pink, yellow; crochet hooks size E, D and C *or the sizes that will give you the correct gauge;* 2 yards 30"-wide silk lining; 1 yd narrow elastic; 2½ yds 1½"-wide grosgrain ribbon; hook and eye.

Gauge Large square made with size E hook measures 3¼"; medium square made with size D hook measures 2¾"; small square made with size C hook measures 2½.

NOTE: Skirt is made of 154 [165—176] squares joined into 11 rings of 14 [15—16] squares each. Use size E hook for first 4 rings, size D hook for next 4 rings, size C hook for top 3 rings. Make squares in varying combinations of 3 colors on first 3 rnds, using MC for the 4th rnd only on all squares.

First Square With first color and size E hook, starting at center ch 5. Join with sl st to form ring.

1st rnd With same color, ch 4, work 2 tr in ring, ch 2 (3 tr in ring, ch 2) 3 times; join with sl st to top of first ch-4. Break off.

2nd rnd Attach 2nd color to any ch-2 sp, ch 4, work 2 tr, ch 2 and 3 tr in same sp, (ch 1, 3 tr, ch 2 and 3 tr in next corner sp) 3 times; ch 1; join with sl st to top of first ch-4. Break off.

3rd rnd Attach 3rd color to any corner sp, ch 4, work 2 tr, ch 2 and 3 tr in same sp (first corner), * ch 1, 3 tr in next ch-1 sp, ch 1, work 3 tr, ch 2 and 3 tr in next sp, ch 1 (next corner). Repeat from * twice more, ch 1, 3 tr in next ch-1 sp, ch 1; join with sl st to top of first ch-4. Break off.

4th rnd Attach MC to any corner sp and work a first corner in same sp, * (ch 1, 3 tr in next ch-1 sp) twice; ch 1, work corner in next corner sp. Repeat from * twice more; (ch 1, 3 tr in next ch-1 sp) twice, ch 1; join with sl st to first ch-4. Break off.

Second Square Using other colors, work first 3 rnds as on first square.

4th rnd Attach MC to any corner sp, work a first corner in same sp, (ch 1, 3 tr in next ch-1 sp) twice; ch 1, 3 tr in next corner, drop lp from hook, place first and second squares wrong sides tog, pull lp through corner sp of first square, ch 2, 3 tr in same corner on second square, (ch 1, drop lp and pull through next ch-1 sp on first square, 3 tr in next ch-1 sp on second square) twice, ch 1; join to next ch-1 sp on first square; 3 tr in next corner on second square, join to corner on first square, ch 2, 3 tr in same corner on second square (1 side joined), complete 4th rnd as on first square.

1st ring Make 12 (13—14) squares more in same manner as second square, using as many color combinations as possible and arranging them to give a scattered effect, joining each square to preceding one and last square to first square to form a ring.

2nd ring Work as for first ring using different color combinations, joining each square to corresponding square on preceding ring. Work 9 more rings in same manner as second ring (see NOTE for hook sizes).

Waist With size D hook attach double strands of MC to corner sp on last rnd of any square, ch 22, 1 dc in same sp, * (sk 1 tr, 1 dc in next tr, sk 1 tr, 1 dc in ch-1 sp) 3 times, sk 1 tr, 1 dc in next tr, sk 1 tr, ch 22, 1 dc in corner, ch 22, 1 dc in corner of next square. Repeat from * around, ending 1 dc, ch 22, 1 dc in same corner, ch 10, turn.

Next row 2 dc in first lp, * ch 3, 2 dc in next lp. Repeat from * across, ch 2, turn.

Next row Dc in each st across. Break off.

Bottom Border NOTE: Change colors on every rnd as shown, using MC for last rnd. With size E hook, attach yarn to corner of any square, ch 4, work 2 tr in same sp, * (ch 1, 3 tr in next ch-1 sp) 3 times, ch 1, 3 tr in next corner, ch 1, 3 tr in corner on next square. Repeat from * around, ending 3 tr in corner, ch 1, join with sl st to top of ch-4. Break off.

2nd rnd Attach another color yarn to any ch-1 sp, ch 4, 2 tr in same sp, * ch 1, 3 tr in next ch-1 sp. Repeat from * around, ending ch 1, join with sl st to top of first ch-4. Break off. Repeat 2nd rnd until 40" from waist or desired length.

Finishing Cut 2 pieces of lining to fit shape of back and front, allowing for seams, a 2½" hem at bottom and a little fullness. Sew seams, leaving a 2½" opening at top left seam. Hem around opening. Ease top edge of lining to top of last rnd of squares. Sew in place. Cut elastic to fit waist and sew to top of lining; upper edge is left free. Sew on hook and eye. Turn up hem. Draw ribbon through loops at waist as shown.

MOSAIC SKIRT

The dramatic look and vivid stained-glass colors of these squares should make this skirt a fireside favorite for years to come. The grannies are especially quick to work because they're made with a large hook and a fairly heavy yarn. And it's designed for one size, fitting almost anyone.

Size One size fits all.

Materials Bernat Sesame, 2 ounces each orange, emerald, fuchsia, heliotrope, black; crochet hook size G *or size that will give you the correct gauge;* tapestry needle.

Colors Make 8 squares of each color combination working 1 rnd of each color; make 8 triangles, following directions below.

Square 1 Orange, heliotrope, fuchsia, emerald.

Square 2 Heliotrope, fuchsia, emerald, orange.

Square 3 Emerald, fuchsia, heliotrope, orange.

Square 4 Fuchsia, emerald, orange, heliotrope.

Square 5 Orange, emerald, fuchsia, heliotrope.

Square 6 Fuchsia, heliotrope, orange, emerald.

Square 7 Emerald, orange, heliotrope, fuchsia.

Triangles Heliotrope, orange, emerald, fuchsia.

Squares With first color, starting at center, ch 4. Join with sl st to form ring.

1st rnd Ch 3 (count ch-3 as first dc), work 2 dc in ring, (ch 3, 3 dc in ring) 3 times; ch 3; join with sl st to top of ch-3. Break off.

2nd rnd Join 2nd color in any ch-3 sp, ch 4, dc in same sp, * (ch 1, sk next dc, dc in next sp between dcs) twice, ch 1, sk next dc, (dc, ch 3 and dc) in next ch-3 sp (corner sp). Repeat from * twice more, ending (ch 1, sk next dc, dc in next sp between dcs) twice, ch 1; join to 3rd ch of ch-4. Break off.

3rd rnd Join 3rd color in any ch-3 corner sp, ch 3, in same sp work 2 dc, ch 2 and 3 dc (first corner), * sk 2 dc, 3 dc in next sp, sk 2 dc, in next corner sp work 3 dc, ch 2 and 3 dc (another corner). Repeat from * twice more, ending sk 2 dc, 3 dc in next sp, sk 2 dc; join. Break off.

4th rnd Join 4th color in any ch-2 corner sp and work a first corner in same sp, * (sk next 3 dc, 3 dc in next sp) twice, sk 3 dc, work another corner in next ch-2 corner sp. Repeat from * twice more, ending (sk next 3 dc, 3 dc in next sp) twice; join. Break off.

Triangles With first color, ch 4, join with sl st to form ring.
1st row Ch 3, 9 dc in ring (10 dc, counting ch-3 as 1 dc). Do not join. Break off.
2nd row Join 2nd color in top of ch-3, ch 4, dc in ch-3 lp, ch 1, dc in first sp between dcs, * ch 1, sk next dc, dc in next sp. Repeat from * around (10 dc). Break off.
3rd row Join 3rd color in 3rd ch of ch-4, ch 3, 3 dc in first sp, sk next 2 dc, 3 dc in next sp, sk next 2 dc, work 3 dc, ch 2 and 3 dc in next sp (corner sp), (sk next 2 dc, 3 dc in next sp) twice, dc in last dc. Break off.
4th row Join 4th color in top of ch-3, ch 3, 3 dc in sp between ch-3 and first dc, (sk 3 dc, 3 dc in next sp) twice; sk 3 dc, work 3 dc, ch 2 and 3 dc in ch-2 corner sp, (sk 3 dc, 3 dc in next sp) 3 times, dc in last dc. Break off.
Finishing: Edging With black, right side facing, join yarn in any st, ch 1, sc in sp between each two stitches of square, working 3 sc in each corner sp; join. Break off. Work same edging around each square and each triangle.
Joining With black and right side facing, working under 2 top lps of each st, sew squares together. Squares 1 form lower edge, 2 the row above, and so on; triangles are used at top of skirt.
Waistband With black, join yarn in any st, ch 4, * sk 1 sc, dc in next sc, ch 1. Repeat from * around; join in 3rd ch of ch-4.
2nd rnd Ch 4, dc in first sp, * ch 1, dc in next sp. Repeat from * around; join in 3rd ch of ch-4. Repeat the last rnd 3 times more. Break off.
Ties (make 3) With double strands of black make a chain to measure approximately 100″. To insert tie, run it through last rnd of crochet by inserting it from front to back, starting at center front; work under 1 dc and over 3 dc around top of skirt. Working in every other rnd, run remaining ties through waistband in same manner.
Fringe Cut strands of black 8″ long. Knot 3 strands in every other st around lower edge of skirt. Trim ends.

FLOPPY HAT

Thick glossy yellow and orange rug yarn makes a brilliant, casual hat. Crown is granny-squared. The scalloped brim is single crochet and can be deftly turned back or worn down in your best Garboesque manner.

Size Fits head 20" to 22".

Materials Aunt Lydia's heavy rug yarn, 2 (70-yard) skeins bongo (dark orange) No. 224 (color A) , 1 skein orange No. 226 (B); aluminum crochet hook size H *or the size that will give you the correct gauge;* tapestry needle.

Gauge On brim, 3 sc=1"; 3 rows=1". Each square measures 4" x 4½".

Top of Crown Starting at top with color A, ch 4. Join with sl st to form ring. **1st rnd** Work 7 sc in ring. Do not join rnds but mark beg of each rnd. **2nd rnd** Work 2 sc in each sc around (14 sc). **3rd rnd** * Sc in next sc, 2 sc in next sc. Repeat from * around (21 sc). Continue in this manner for 4 rnds more, increasing 7 sc, evenly spaced, on each rnd (49 sc). Piece should measure about 5¼" in diameter. Break off A; attach B. **8th rnd** Dc in each sc around, increasing 6 dc as evenly spaced as possible (55 dc). **9th rnd** Sc in each dc around; join. Break off.

Squares (make 4) Starting at center with B, ch 4. Join with sl st to form ring.

1st rnd Ch 3, work 2 dc in ring (ch 1, 3-dc shell in ring) 3 times; ch 1; join with sl st to top of ch-3. Break off.

2nd rnd With A sl st in any ch-1 sp, ch 3, in same sp work 2 dc, ch 1 and 3 dc (first corner), * ch 1, in next ch-1 sp work 3 dc, ch 1 and 3 dc (another corner). Repeat from * twice more; ch 1; join.

3rd rnd Sl st to next ch-1 corner sp, work 3 sc in corner sp, work sc in each dc and ch-1 sp around, working 3 sc in each remaining corner sp; sc in 2 sc sts at beg of rnd; join with sl st to first sc. Break off.

4th rnd With B sl st in any corner sc, ch 3, work 10 dc along 1 edge only. Break off. This will produce a slightly rectangular shape.

To Assemble Crown To join, hold 2 squares with wrong sides facing. With B, whipstitch 4th row edge (color B) on 1 square to

an A edge on adjacent square. Join squares to form ring. With B, whipstitch crown to one edge of ring.

Brim: 1st rnd With right side of crown facing you, using B, work 58 sc, evenly spaced, along lower edge of crown; join. Break off. **2nd rnd** With A, sl st in first sc, ch 3, dc in same sc, * dc in next sc, 2 dc in next sc. Repeat from * around (88 dc); join. **3rd rnd** Sc in each dc around, increasing 3 sc as evenly spaced as possible (91 sc). **4th through 7th rnds** Sc in each sc around. **8th rnd (scalloped edge)** * Sk 2 sc, work 6 dc in next sc, sk 2 sc, sc in next sc. Repeat from * around; join. Break off. **9th rnd** With B, work sc in each st around. Break off.

COLD-WEATHER HELMET

*To keep the chill winds from whistling down your ski jacket here's
a gay helmet that fits right down to the shoulders and ties in place.
Some of the grannies have one round of angora yarn to give an unusual contrast of textures.*

Size Fits 22" head.

Materials Knitting worsted, 4 ounces royal blue, small
amounts rainbow ombré, purple, red, rose, gold and bright
green; small amount white angora; aluminum crochet hook
size G *or the size that will give you the correct gauge;* tapestry
needle.

Gauge 4 sts = 1"; 3 rows = 2".

Crown Starting at top with blue, ch 6. Join with sl st to form
ring.

1st rnd Ch 3, work 15 dc in ring (16 dc, counting ch-3 as 1 dc);
join with sl st in top of ch-3. Break off blue; attach purple.

2nd rnd Ch 5, * dc in next dc, ch 2. Repeat from * around;
join with sl st in 3rd ch of ch-5. Break off purple; attach red.

3rd rnd Sl st in next ch-2 sp, ch 3, dc in same sp, ch 2, * 2 dc in
next ch-2 sp, ch 2. Repeat from * around; join. Break off red;
attach blue.

4th rnd Repeat 3rd rnd. Break off blue; attach rose.

5th rnd Sl st in next ch-2 sp, ch 5, dc in sp between next 2 dc, *
ch 2, dc in next ch-2 sp, ch 2, dc in sp between next 2 dc. Repeat
from * around, ch 2; join in 3rd ch of ch-5. Break off rose; attach blue.

6th rnd Repeat 3rd rnd. Break off blue; attach red.

7th rnd Sl st in next ch-2 sp, ch 4, dc in sp between next 2 dc, ch
1, * dc in next ch-2 sp, ch 1, dc in sp between next 2 dc, ch 1. Repeat from * around; join in 3rd ch of ch-4. Break off red; attach
blue.

8th rnd Sl st in next ch-1 sp, ch 4, * dc in next ch-1 sp, ch 1. Repeat from * around; join in 3rd ch of ch-4.

9th rnd Sl st in next sp, ch 3, work 4 dc in same sp, sk next 2 sp,
* work 5 dc in next sp, sk next 2 sp. Repeat from * around;
join. Break off.

Flap Work 2 granny squares in each of the following color
combinations (1 rnd of each color): **Square 1—** gold, angora

and blue; **Square 2**—red, angora and blue; **Square 3**— ombré, green and blue; **Square 4**—ombré, red and blue; **Square 5**—yellow, ombré and blue.

Squares Starting at center, ch 4. Join with sl st to form ring.

1st rnd Ch 3, work 2 dc in ring, (ch 1, 3-dc shell in ring) 3 times; ch 1; join with sl st to top of ch-3. Break off.

2nd rnd Sl st in any ch-1 sp, ch 3, in same sp work 2 dc, ch 1 and 3 dc (first corner), * ch 1, in next ch-1 sp work 3 dc, ch 1 and 3 dc (another corner). Repeat from * twice more; ch 1; join. Break off.

3rd rnd Sl st in any ch-1 corner sp and work a first corner in same sp, * ch 1, 3-dc shell in next ch-1 sp, ch 1, work corner in next corner sp. Repeat from * twice more; ch 1, shell in next sp, ch 1; join. Break off.

With right sides facing, working with blue through back lps only, whipstitch squares tog to complete flap, following diagram for placement.

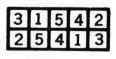

HELMET FLAP

Finishing Whipstitch upper edge of flap to lower edge of crown in same manner as for squares, leaving 10″ of crown free for face edge. With right side facing you, attach blue to corner joining of flap to crown at left temple. Work 5-dc shell in corner joining, sl st in back lp of 3rd st on side edge of flap. Break off. Work 5-dc shell in joining at right temple.

Ties With blue, crochet 2 chains 8″ long. Attach to lower front corner of flap on each side and tie in bow.

SNUGGLY BONNET

*Any little girl would love this snuggly bonnet for blustery win-
ter days. It's great when you're building a snowman. Just four
grannies edged with single crochet form the bonnet. The ties
are worked right in with the edging. The perky little bobbles
are sewed in place.*

Size Fits 19″ head.
Materials Knitting worsted, 2 ounces main color (color A), 1
ounce each B and C; aluminum crochet hook size G *or the size
that will give you the correct gauge;* tapestry needle.
Gauge Each square measures 4½″.
Squares (make 4) Starting at center with A, ch 6. Join with sl st
to form ring.
1st rnd Ch 3, work 2 dc in ring, (ch 1, 3 dc in ring) 3 times; ch 1;
join with sl st to top of ch-3. Break off.
2nd rnd Attach B with sl st in any ch-1 sp, ch 3, in same sp
work 2 dc, ch 1 and 3 dc (first corner), * ch 1, in next ch sp
work 3 dc, ch . and 3 dc (another corner). Repeat from * twice
more; ch 1; join with sl st to top of ch-3. Break off.
3rd rnd Attach C to any ch-1 corner sp and work a first corner
in same sp, * ch 1, 3 dc in next ch-1 sp (shell made), ch 1, work
corner in next corner sp. Repeat from * twice more; ch 1, shell
in next sp, ch 1; join. Break off.
4th rnd Attach A in any corner sp and work a first corner in
same sp, * (ch 1, shell in next ch-1 sp) twice; ch 1, work corner
in next corner sp. Repeat from * twice more; (ch 1, shell in
next sp) twice; ch 1; join. Break off.
Finishing With right sides up, sew 3 squares in a row through
top lps only. This forms sides and top of bonnet. Sew 4th
square for back.
Edging With A, work 1 sc in each st and in each seam around
(94 sc); join.
2nd rnd Ch 1, sc in each sc around, decreasing 6 sts, as evenly
spaced as possible, along back edge only (47 sts on front, 41 sts
on back).
3rd rnd Ch 1, sc in each sc around, decreasing 4 sts, evenly
spaced, along front edge and 6 sts, evenly spaced, along back
edge; join.

4th rnd Ch 1, sc in each sc around, decreasing 4 sts along front edge and 6 sts along back edge (39 sts on front edge, 29 sts on back edge). Do not break off. Ch 41 for tie, sc in 2nd ch from hook and in each ch across; with right side facing you, sc in each sc across back edge, ch 41 for 2nd tie, sc in 2nd ch from hook and in each ch across; sl st in bonnet. Break off.

Bobbles (make 8) With C, ch 2, work 5 sc in 2nd ch from hook, ch 1, turn.

2nd through 4th rows Sc in each sc across; ch 1, turn.

5th row (Insert hook in next sc, pull yarn through) 5 times; y o hook and pull through all 6 lps on hook. Break off, leaving a 6" end. Thread end in tapestry needle and run through edges of bobbles; pull tight. Sew on front edging as shown in photograph.

GIRL'S HEADHUGGER

Ears are guaranteed to stay warm under this quick-to-make head-hugger. If you have any granny squares left over from an afghan or other project, this is an ideal way to use them up. Just be sure that you have enough yarn to finish the crown.

Materials Knitting worsted, 1 ounce each white (color A), red (B), magenta (C) and purple (D); aluminum crochet hook size F *or the size that will give you the correct gauge;* tapestry needle.
Gauge Each square measures 4¼". On crown: 7 h dc = 2".
Squares (make 2) Starting at center with A, ch 4. Join with sl st to form ring.
1st rnd (right side) Ch 2, 1 h dc in ring, (ch 2, 2 h dc in ring) 3 times; ch 2; join with sl st to top of ch-2. Break off.
2nd rnd Attach B with sl st to any ch-2 sp, ch 2, in same sp work 1 h dc, ch 2 and 2 h dc (first corner), * 1 h dc in each of next 2 sts, in next ch-2 sp work 2 h dc, ch 2 and 2 h dc (another corner). Repeat from * twice more; h dc in each of next 2 sts; join with sl st to top of ch-2. From now on, corners are worked differently.
3rd rnd Attach A to any corner sp, ch 3, in same sp work 1 h dc (first corner), * 1 h dc in each of next 6 h dc, in next corner sp work 1 h dc, ch 2 and 1 h dc (another corner). Repeat from * twice more; 1 h dc in each of next 6 h dc; join with sl st to 2nd ch of ch-3. Break off.
4th rnd Attach C to any corner sp, work as for 3rd rnd, working 2 more h dc between each corner. Break off.
5th rnd With color D, work as for 4th rnd.
6th rnd With color B, work as for 4th rnd.
Crown With B, ch 32 to measure 9".
1st row Work 1 h dc in third ch from hook and in each ch across (30 h dc plus turning ch). Ch 2, turn.
2nd row Work 1 h dc in each h dc across. Ch 2, turn. Repeat 2nd row 4 times more. Break off B. Continue to work in same manner, working one row each of A, C, D, B, D, C and A, then work 6 rows more with B. Break off.
Finishing Place one square at each narrow end of crown. One corner of square will slightly overlap. Sew in place.

Ties (make 2) With two strands of color B, make ch to measure 11". Break off.

Tassels (make 2) For each one: Cut 6 strands each of A, B, C and D, 6" long. With B, tie tog tightly at center, leaving 6" ends of B. Fold strands in half and, with B, tie tog again ¾" below fold. Using 6" end of B, sew to crocheted tie.

Sew crocheted ties to headhugger.

HEAD-TURNING BERET

A six-sided granny forms the center of this jaunty beret. Six traditional grannies and a single-crochet headband complete the hat. It takes so little time and is such fun to make that you'll soon have a whole wardrobe of berets to go with every outfit.

Size Fits about 22" head size.

Materials Lily Sugar-'n'-Cream cotton yarn, 2 (125-yard) balls dark rose No. 44 (color D), 1 ball each red No. 95 (R), orange No. 20 (0), medium blue No. 29 (B) and turquoise No. 36 (T); aluminum crochet hooks sizes E and F *or the sizes that will give you the correct gauge.*

NOTE: Beret is composed of 6 squares, 1 hexagon and headband.

Gauge Hexagon measures 7" from a corner to opposite corner. Each square measures 5".

Hexagon Starting at center with D and size E hook, ch 8. Join with sl st to form ring.

1st rnd Ch 3, 2 dc in ring, (ch 1, 3 dc in ring) 5 times, ch 1; join with sl st to top of ch-3. Break off.

2nd rnd With T sl st in any ch-1 sp, ch 3, work 2 dc, ch 1 and 3 dc for first corner, * ch 1, in next sp work 3 dc, ch 1 and 3 dc (another corner). Repeat from * 4 times more (6 corners); ch 1, join. Break off.

3rd rnd With R , work first corner in any corner sp, * ch 1, 3-dc shell in next sp, ch 1, work corner in next corner sp. Repeat from * 4 times more; ch 1, shell in next sp, ch 1; join. Break off.

4th rnd With B, work first corner in any corner sp, * (ch 1, shell in next sp) twice; ch 1, corner in next corner sp. Repeat from * 4 times more; (ch 1, shell in next sp) twice ch 1; join. Break off.

5th rnd With D, work first corner in any corner sp, * (ch 1, shell in next sp) 3 times; ch 1, corner in next corner sp. Repeat from * 4 times more; (ch 1, shell in next sp) 3 times, ch 1; join. Break off.

Squares (make 6) Starting at center, with size E hook, ch 6. Join with sl st to form ring.

1st rnd Ch 3, work 2 dc in ring, (ch 1, 3-dc shell in ring) 3 times; ch 1; join with sl st to top of ch-3. Break off.

2nd rnd Sl st in any ch 1 sp, ch 3, in same sp work 2 dc, ch 1 and 3 dc (first corner), * ch-1, in next ch-1 sp work 3 dc, ch 1 and 3 dc (another corner). Repeat from * twice more; ch 1; join. Break off.

3rd rnd Sl st in any ch-1 corner sp and work a first corner in same sp, * ch 1, 3-dc shell in next ch-1 sp, ch 1, work corner in next corner sp. Repeat from * twice more; ch 1, shell in next sp, ch 1; join. Break off.

4th rnd Sl st in any ch-1 corner sp and work a first corner in same sp, * (ch 1, shell in next ch-1 sp) twice; ch 1, work corner in next corner sp. Repeat from * twice more; (ch 1, shell in next sp) twice; ch 1; join. Break off.

5th rnd Sl st in any ch-1 corner sp and work a first corner in same sp, * ch 1, work shell in next ch-1 sp. Repeat from * to next corner, ch 1, work a corner in next corner sp. Continue around in pattern; join. Break off.

Work 1 rnd of each color in each square as follows: **Square 1**—D, O, D, T, D. **Square 2**—D, T, D , B, D. **Square 3**—D, R, D, O, D. **Square 4**—D, T, D, R, D. **Square 5**—D, B, D, O , D. **Square 6** —D, R, D, B, D.

Joining Hold 2 squares with wrong sides together. Using D and size E hook sc through both lps of matching sts along one side. Break off. Join 3rd square to 2nd square, 4th to 3rd, 5th to 4th and 6th to 5th so that piece forms strip. Join ends of strip to form ring.

Join hexagon with sc around 1 edge of ring, joining each section of hexagon to edge of a square. Break off.

Headband 1st rnd With size E hook and D , sc in each st around edge of beret. Count sts. **2nd (dec) rnd** Sc in each sc around, decreasing as evenly as possible, until 56 sts remain (to dec 1 sc, sk 1 sc and sc in next sc). Do not break off; attach another strand D and, using size F hook and marking beg of each rnd, work sc with double yarn in each sc around until headband measures about 1½". Sl st in next sc and break off.

CAP AND SCARF SET

Just five granny squares make the snug little cap. Whipped up in no time, it's a great item for your next bazaar. For a special gift, add the matching scarf with its multicolored tassels. Instead of using four different colors, try four shades of one lovely color.

Size Cap fits head 20″ to 22″. Scarf measures 13½″ by 56″ without tassels.

Materials. Fleisher's knitting worsted, for cap and scarf together, 1 (4-ounce) skein each flaming pink No. 463 (color A), peacock blue No. 473 (B), copper No. 430 (C) and yellow No. 154 (D); aluminum crochet hook size H *or the size that will give you the correct gauge;* tapestry needle.

Gauge Each square measures about 4¼″.

Cap

Squares (make 5) Work first 3 rnds for each square, using A, B or C as desired.

Starting at center, ch 6. Join with sl st to form ring.

1st rnd Ch 3, work 2 dc in ring, (ch 2, 3-dc shell in ring) 3 times; ch 2; join with sl st to top of ch-3. Break off.

2nd rnd Sl st in any ch-2 sp, ch 3, in same sp work 2 dc, ch 2 and 3 dc (first corner), * ch 2, in next ch-2 sp work 3 dc, ch 2 and 3 dc (another corner). Repeat from * twice more; ch 2; join. Break off.

3rd rnd Sl st in any ch-2 corner sp and work a first corner in same sp, * ch 2, 3-dc shell in next ch-2 sp, ch 2, work corner in next corner sp. Repeat from * twice more; ch 2, shell in next sp, ch 2; join. Break off.

4th rnd (border rnd) With D, work sc in each dc and ch st around, working 2 sc in each corner ch st; join. Break off.

To Assemble To join, hold 2 squares with right sides facing. Whipstitch them tog along one edge, working through 1 lp only of each st (ridges formed on right side). Join 4 squares to form ring. Whipstitch remaining square around 1 edge of ring to form top of cap, easing edges to fit smoothly.

Around lower edge of cap, crochet a rnd of 72 sc with D, then 1 rnd each with C, A, B, D and C.

Scarf

Squares (make 36) See squares for cap. Work in an assortment of color combinations, using A, B and C. Use D for sc border on each square.

To Assemble Join squares as for Cap, assembling them 3 squares wide by 12 squares long. With D, work sc in each sc around entire scarf, working 3 sc in each corner; join. Break off. At each end of scarf, work 1 row each of C, B, A and D sc.

Next row With C, sl st in first sc of last row, * ch 2, sk next sc, sc in next sc. Repeat from * across.

Tassels Cut one 16″ strand of each color for each tassel. Hold strands tog and fold in half. Draw folded end through first ch-2 sp at end of scarf, then draw ends through lp at folded end; tighten. Attach tassel in each sp across ends of scarf.

SUPER TOTE

*Just three skeins of rug yarn make this sturdy shoulder bag that
will hold everything from baby bottles to your crocheting–more
granny squares? Double the size and you'll have a great bag to tote
on weekends.*

Size About 10" x 14".

Materials Melrose rug yarn, 3 (4-ounce) skeins beige; aluminum crochet hooks sizes H and K *or the size that will give you the
correct gauge;* tapestry needle.

Gauge Each square measures 4¼".

Squares (make 12) Starting at center, with H hook, ch 4. Join
with sl st to form ring.

1st rnd Ch 3, work 2 dc in ring (ch 2, 3-dc shell in ring) 3 times;
ch 2; join with sl st to top of ch-3.

2nd rnd Ch 3, 1 dc in each of next 2 dc; (in corner sp work 2 dc,
ch 2 and 2 dc; 1 dc in each of next 3 dc) 3 times; in corner sp
work 2 dc, ch 2 and 2 dc; join.

3rd rnd Ch 3, 1 dc in each of next 4 dc; (in corner sp work 2 dc,
ch 2 and 2 dc; 1 dc in each of next 7 dc) 3 times; in corner sp
work 2 dc, ch 2 and 2 dc; 1 dc in each of next 2 dc; join. Break
off.

To Assemble With wrong sides tog join squares with sc. Make
2 rows of 3 squares each for front of tote. Join the 2 rows tog
with sc. Repeat for back of tote.

Gusset With H hook ch 6. Sc in 2nd ch from hook and in each
ch across (5 sc), ch 1, turn. Sc in each sc across, ch 1, turn. Repeat until gusset measures long enough to go around sides and
lower edge of bag plus 9" (about 116 rows). Fold gusset crosswise to find center. Center the center of gusset on lower edge of
front of tote. Pin gusset in place. Starting at upper right corner,
join with sc. At upper left corner do not break off but continue
across top with sc in every st, also working 1 sc in every corner
sp and in joinings between squares; join. Break off. Repeat for
back of tote. Fold gusset extensions to inside of tote and sew in
place.

Handle With K hook and yarn double, make a ch 66" long.
Break off. Thread ch through gusset extensions. Sew ends
together.

PERIPATETIC POUCH BAG

Five 12" grannies join forces for a great hold-everything pouch. Slung on two crocheted straps it will be the handiest bag you've ever had.

Size About 12" square.

Materials Aunt Lydia's heavy rug yarn, 4 (70-yard) skeins burnt orange No. 320; Dawn Wintuk sport yarn, 3 (2-ounce) skeins grape spice No. 60, 1 skein each black No. 70, red spice No. 20 and flame No. 15; aluminum crochet hook size G *or the size that will give you the correct gauge;* tapestry needle; ¾ yard 45"-wide muslin for lining.

Gauge Each square measures 12".

NOTE: When working with rug yarn, use 1 strand; when working with sport yarn, use 3 strands held together.

Squares (make 5) Starting at center, ch 6. Join with sl st to form ring.

1st rnd Ch 3, work 2 dc in ring, (ch 1, 3-dc shell in ring) 3 times; ch 1; join with sl st to top of ch-3. Break off.

2nd rnd Sl st in any ch 1 sp, ch 3, in same sp work 2 dc, ch 1 and 3 dc (first corner), * ch 1, in next ch-1 sp work 3 dc, ch 1 and 3 dc (another corner). Repeat from * twice more; ch 1; join. Break off.

3rd rnd Sl st in any ch-1 corner sp and work a first corner in same sp, * ch 1, 3-dc shell in next ch-1 sp, ch 1, work corner in next corner sp. Repeat from * twice more; ch 1, shell in next sp, ch 1; join. Break off.

4th rnd Sl st in any ch-1 corner sp and work a first corner in same sp, * (ch 1, shell in next ch-1 sp) twice; ch 1, work corner in next corner sp. Repeat from * twice more; (ch 1, shell in next sp) twice; ch 1; join. Break off.

5th rnd Sl st in any ch-1 corner sp and work a first corner in same sp, * ch 1, work shell in next ch-1 sp. Repeat from * to next corner, ch 1, work a corner in next corner sp. Continue around in pattern; join. Break off.

Repeat last rnd 4 more times (9 rnds in all).

Work in the following color sequence: 2 rnds orange, 2 rnds grape spice, 1 rnd each orange and black, 1 rnd of 2 stands flame and 1 strand red spice held tog, 1 rnd each grape spice and orange. For directions on how to work consecutive rnds with the same color, see "Changing Colors", page 140.

Joining Hold 2 squares with wrong sides tog. With orange, work sc through both lps of matching sts along one side. Join 3rd square to 2nd square and 4th to 3rd so that piece forms strip; then join ends of strip to form ring. Matching corners, join remaining square around one edge of ring to form bottom of bag.

Lining Cut 5 squares muslin same size as granny squares, adding ½" seam allowance to all edges. Sew muslin squares tog in same shape as bag. Place lining in bag, wrong sides tog. Turn under seam allowance one row from top edge of bag. Matching lining seams to bag seams, blindstitch around top edge. Working from right side, tack lining to bottom corners of bag.

Straps With orange, crochet 38" chain. Sc in 2nd ch from hook and in each ch across; continuing around chain, work sc in each st across opposite edge of chain; sl st in first sc. Break off. At top of bag, thread strap through corner of one square and through corner of adjoining 2nd square. Pulling strap through, thread same end at top edge through opposite corner of 2nd square and through adjoining corner of 3rd square. Sew ends of strap tog with yarn and tapestry needle.

Make another strap and insert it in same manner through corners on opposite side of bag. Sew ends tog. With straps parallel and seams matching sew tog for 8" to form broad section for shoulder.

Victorian vest, page 17

ild's patchwork sweater, page 33

Rosetted belt, page 65

Mosaic skirt, page 41

Floppy hat, page 43

Peripatetic pouch bag, page 6

Out-of-the-blue jacket, page 13

Surefooted slippers, page 72

Diamond Jim tie, page 69 ▶

Cold weather helmet, page 47

Putting-on-the-dog coat, page 74

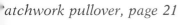

atchwork pullover, page 21

Rugged hearth rug (detail), page 93

Out-of-the-blue jacket (detail), page 13

Different shapes to create, pages 148ff.

Hail to the hassock (detail), page 97

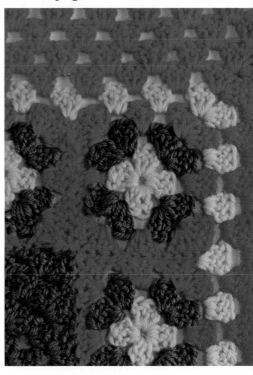

Out-of-the-ordinary crib afghan (detail), page 87

ap and scarf set (detail), page 57

Diamond Jim tie (detail), page 69

Flamboyant afghan, page 76

Rugged hearth rug, page 93

Pretty pillow, page 99

Hail to the hassock, page 97

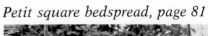
Petit square bedspread, page 81

Dream-of-a-bedspread, page 83

Rustic place mat, page 90

ROSETTED BELT

Although this belt is far from the traditional granny look, it is actually nine squares—all a simple variation on the granny. The extra petals in the center of every other unit are Irish crochet—easier than you think. For perfect fit, add or subtract squares. The belt ties in back or front, as you like.

Size 3" wide. Length is adjustable.

Materials Brunswick Coolspun (a nubby bouclé-type yarn), 1 (1-ounce) skein each of carrot No. 1113 (color C), old lace No. 1101 (0), Jamaica No. 1178 (J) and marigold No. 1190 (M); aluminum crochet hook size G *or the size that will give you the correct gauge.*

Gauge Each square measures 2¾".

Rosetted Squares (Make 4 squares, working 2 with color C for rnds 1 through 5 and 2 with J for rnds 1 through 5. Work rnds 6 and 7 with 0).

Starting at center, ch 6. Join with sl st to form ring.

1st rnd Work (sc, 3 dc and sc) 4 times in ring (4 petals).

2nd rnd (Ch 4, sk next sc and 3 dc, sl st in next sc) 4 times; push chains behind petals.

3rd rnd Work sc, 5 dc and sc over each ch (4 petals).

4th rnd (Ch 5, sk next sc and 5 dc, sl st in next sc) 4 times; push chains behind petals.

5th rnd Work sc, 7 dc and sc over each ch (4 petals); join with sl st in first sc. Break off.

6th rnd Sl st in center dc of a petal on last rnd, ch 3, work 2 dc, ch 1 and 3 dc in same dc, * ch 1, 3 dc in next sc, ch 1, work 3 dc, ch 1 and 3 dc in center dc of next petal. Repeat from * twice more; ch 1, 3 dc in next sc, ch 1; join with sl st in top of ch-3.

7th rnd Sc in each dc and ch-1 sp around, working 3 sc in each corner sp; join with sl st in top of ch-3. Break off.

Plain Squares (Make 5 squares, working all rnds with M.)

NOTE: For a longer belt, make additional squares.

Starting at center, ch 4. Join with sl st to form ring.

1st rnd Ch 3, work 11 dc in ring; join with sl st in top of ch-3 (12 dc, counting ch-3 as 1 dc).

2nd rnd (Ch 4, sk next 2 dc, sc in next dc) 4 times (4 lps).

3rd rnd Sl st in next lp, ch 3, work 2 dc, ch 1 and 3 dc in same lp

(first corner), ch 1, * work 3 dc, ch 1 and 3 dc in next lp (another corner), ch 1. Repeat from * twice more; join with sl st in top of ch-3.

4th rnd Sl st to next ch-1 corner sp, work a first corner in same sp, * ch 1, 3 dc in next ch-1 sp, ch 1, work corner in next corner sp. Repeat from * twice more, ch 1, 3 dc in next ch-1 sp, ch 1; join.

5th rnd Sc in each dc and ch-1 sp around, working 3 sc in each corner sp; join with sl st in first sc. Break off.

Finishing Pin squares tog, right side up, in the following order: Plain Square, Rosetted Square with color C, Plain Square, Rosetted Square with color J, Plain Square, Rosetted Square with C, Plain Square, Rosetted Square with color J, Plain Square. With color J, sl st squares tog from right side so that ridge forms. With right side facing and using M, * work 1 row sc along one long edge of belt, ch 30 for tie, turn, work sc in 2nd ch from hook and in each ch across (tie completed), work sc along short end of belt, make another tie. Repeat from * along remaining 2 sides of belt. Join and break off.

DIAMOND JIM TIE

An amusing man's necktie is made of grannies in the old tra-dition—bright centers, black borders. The squares are tiny two-and-a-half-inch ones and go very quickly. The narrow end of tie is worked in single crochet. Unlike most crocheted ties, this one is lined to facilitate tying.

Materials Brunswick Fairhaven fingering yarn, 2 (1-ounce) skeins black No. 1660 (color A), 1 skein each light yellow No. 1603 (B), Danish blue No. 1684 (C), helio No. 1638 (D), pink No. 1615 (E), absinthe heather No. 1671 (F) and emerald No. 1683 (G); steel crochet hook No. 2 *or the size that will give you the correct gauge;* ¼ yard 44"-wide silk or rayon lining fabric; 1 yard 1½"-wide grosgrain ribbon.

Gauge 8 sc=1"; each square measures 2½".

Squares Use B, C, D or E for first rnd of each square, and for all squares use F for 2nd rnd, G for 3rd rnd and A for 4th rnd. Make 15 squares, using color indicated on each square of assembly diagram for first rnd.

Starting at center, ch 6. Join with sl st to form ring.

1st rnd Ch 3, work 2 dc in ring, (ch 3, 3-dc shell in ring) 3 times; ch 3; join with sl st to top of ch-3. Break off.

2nd rnd Sl st in any ch-3 sp, ch 3, in same sp work 2 dc, ch 3 and 3 dc (first corner), * ch 1, in next ch-3 sp work 3 dc, ch 3 and 3 dc (another corner). Repeat from * twice more; ch 1; join. Break off.

3rd rnd Sl st in any ch-3 corner sp and work a first corner in same sp, * ch 1, 3-dc shell in next ch-1 sp, ch 1, work corner in next corner sp. Repeat from * twice more; ch 1, shell in next sp, ch 1; join. Break off.

4th rnd Sl st in any ch-3 corner sp and work a first corner in same sp, * (ch 1, shell in next ch-1 sp) twice; ch 1, work corner in next corner sp. Repeat from * twice more; (ch 1, shell in next sp) twice; ch 1; join. Break off.

Triangles (make 6) Work 4 rows with A only.

1st row Starting at center of one edge, ch 5; in 5th ch from hook work 3 dc, ch 3, 3 dc, ch 1 and 1 dc. Break off.

2nd row Sl st in first ch-4 lp, ch 4, work 3 dc in same lp, ch 1, in next ch-1 sp work 3 dc, ch 3 and 3 dc (corner), ch 1, in last sp work 3 dc, ch 1 and 1 dc. Break off.

3rd row Sl st in first ch-4 lp, ch 4, 3 dc in same lp, ch 1, 3 dc in next ch-1 sp, ch 1, corner in next ch-3 corner sp, ch 1, 3 dc in next sp, ch 1, in last sp work 3 dc, ch 1 and 1 dc. Break off.

4th row Sl st in first ch-4 lp, ch 4, 3 dc in same lp, (ch 1, 3 dc in next ch-1 sp) twice; ch 1, corner in ch-3 corner sp, (ch 1, 3 dc in next sp) twice; ch 1, in last sp work 3 dc, ch 1 and 1 dc. Break off.

To Assemble Follow assembly diagram for placement of squares and triangles. To join, hold 2 squares with right sides facing and whipstitch along one edge, working through front lp only of each st (ridges formed on right side).

Tie Extension With A, sl st at upper edge of tie (X on diagram).

1st row Work 15 sc evenly across edge to Y; ch 1, turn.

2nd row Sc in 15 sc across; ch 1, turn. Repeat last row until extension measures 10½" from beg.

Next row (dec row) Draw up a lp in each of first 2 sc, y o, draw through all 3 lps on hook (1 dec made), sc in each sc to within last 2 sc, dec 1 sc; ch 1, turn. Work 1 row even, then repeat dec row once more. Work even on 11 sc until extension measures 38" from beg. Dec 1 sc at beg and end of row for next 4 rows (3 sc remain).

Next row Sc across 3 sc. Break off.

Lining Enlarge pattern diagram and cut paper pattern, adding ½" seam allowance to all edges. Cut lining pieces and, with right sides tog, stitch around lower edge and sides, leaving top edge open for turning. Trim seams and turn. Cut grosgrain ribbon to measure 29". Cut one end to a point to correspond to narrow end of tie. Place ribbon along narrow end of tie and sew in place. Center lining between broken lines on wrong side of tie as shown on assembly diagram. Turn in top raw edges and sew lining in place.

Fold sides of tie to back, over lining. The crocheted edges must be cut so that they will butt in order to avoid the extra bulk of a thick seam. Before cutting tie, pin seam, then baste along each pinned line separately, being careful not to run needle through both thicknesses of seam. Remove pins and open tie. Run 2 lines of closely spaced machine stitches (or backstitch by hand) along each basting line. The stitching will keep crochet from raveling when it is cut. Cut seam away close to stitching lines. Butt and whipstitch edges together.

DIAMOND JIM TIE

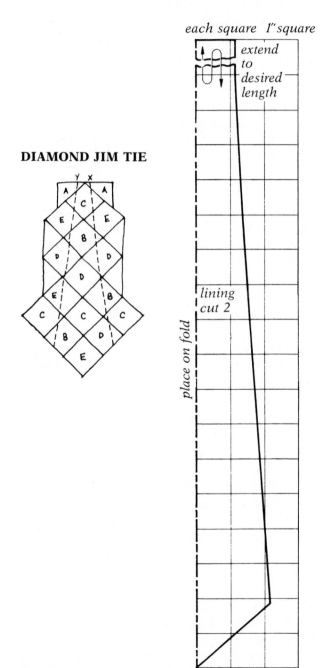

each square 1″ square

SUREFOOTED SLIPPERS

Grannies have gone to your head. Now there's no reason why they can't go to the other extreme—or extremity. A crocheted sole and six little squares form the most comfortable slipper imaginable. A crocheted tie weaves through top of the slipper and holds it neatly in place.

Sizes Sole measures 4″ wide at widest point and about 8½″ [9″ —9½″] long. Slippers are quite stretchy and size is adjustable.
Materials 4 ounces knitting worsted in assorted colors; aluminum crochet hook size G *or the size that will give you the correct gauge.*
Gauge 3 sc on sole=1″; 7 rows=2″.
Soles Choose 2 colors and use 1 strand of each color worked tog. Starting at back of heel, ch 6. **1st row** Sc in 2nd ch from hook and in each ch across (5 sc); ch 1, turn. **2nd row** Work 2 sc in first sc, sc in each sc up to last sc, 2 sc in last sc (7 sc); ch 1, turn. **3rd row** Sc in each sc across; ch 1, turn. **4th row** Repeat 2nd row (9 sc); ch 1, turn. Repeat 3rd row 6 times more. **11th row** Draw up lp in each of first 2 sc, y o and draw through all 3 lps on hook (1 sc dec), sc in each sc up to last 2 sc, dec 1 sc (7 sc); ch 1, turn. Repeat 3rd row 2 [4—6] times. **Next row** Repeat 2nd row (9 sc); ch 1, turn. Repeat 3rd row twice. **Next row** Repeat 2nd row (11 sc); ch 1, turn. Repeat 3rd row 8 times. **Next row** Repeat 11th row (9 sc); ch 1, turn. Repeat 3rd row once. **Next row** Repeat 11th row (7 sc); ch 1, turn. Repeat 3rd row once. **Next row** Repeat 11th row (5 sc). Break off.
Slipper-Top Granny Squares Work with 1 strand yarn. Starting at center, ch 4. Join with sl st to form ring.
1st rnd Ch 3, work 2 dc in ring, (ch 1, 3-dc shell in ring) 3 times; ch 1; join with sl st to top of ch-3. Break off.
2nd rnd Sl st in any ch 1 sp, ch 3, in same sp work 2 dc, ch 1 and 3 dc (first corner), * ch 1, in next ch-1 sp work 3 dc, ch 1 and 3 dc (another corner). Repeat from * twice more; ch 1; join. Break off.
3rd rnd Sl st in any ch-1 corner sp and work a first corner in same sp, * ch 1, 3-dc shell in next ch-1 sp, ch 1, work corner in next corner sp. Repeat from * twice more; ch 1, shell in next sp, ch 1; join. Break off.

Work each rnd in a different color. Completed square

SUREFOOTED SLIPPERS

should measure 3″. Make 11 more squares (6 for each slipper).
To Assemble Choose 6 squares for a slipper and mark them 1 through 6. Hold first and 2nd squares with right sides facing and whipstitch tog along one edge, working through both lps of each st. Open squares out flat. Continue whipstitching squares tog to form a strip (see diagram). Whipstitch edge A of first square to edge B of 6th square. Piece forms ring and 6th square covers instep and toes diagonally.

Pin sole to slipper top, easing or stretching to fit if necessary. Using 1 strand of yarn, sc top to sole, forming ridge around edge.

Top Border Mark center dc on top edge of first and 5th squares. **1st row** Sc in first marked dc, sc in each remaining st of first square, across top edge of 2nd, 3rd and 4th squares and in each st of 5th square to 2nd marked dc; ch 1, turn. **2nd row** Sc in each sc across; ch 3, turn. **3rd row (beading)** Sk first 2 sc, h dc in next sc, * ch 1, sk next sc, h dc in next sc. Repeat from * across. Break off.

Ties Crochet a chain long enough to weave through beading row and tie in a bow. Sc in 2nd ch from hook and in each ch across. Break off.

Assemble other slipper in same manner. Slippers are interchangeable.

PUTTING-ON-THE-DOG COAT

Since this part of Carry-Along Crochet *is all about grannies to wear, it certainly should include something for everyone in the family. Who is more deserving than your loyal tail-wagger? Twenty-eight grannies make this colorful coat for your pet. A special tail-catcher holds it in place no matter how active the dog.*

Size Coat measures 15″ from neck to tail. It can be made larger by adding additional rounds to each square or by adding squares.

Materials Bear Brand Winsom Orlon acrylic yarn, 2 (2-ounce) skeins brick No. 332 (main color), 1 skein each spearmint (light green) No. 367, jubilee jade (dark green) No. 324, sky mist No. 313 and pumpkin No. 302 (P); aluminum crochet hook size E *or the size that will give you the correct gauge;* tapestry needle; 2 buttons 1″ in diameter.

Gauge Each square measures about 3″. 4 sc=1″ on collar.

Squares (make 28) Starting at center, ch 4. Join with sl st to form ring.

1st rnd Ch 3, work 2 dc in ring, (ch 1, 3-dc shell in ring) 3 times; ch 1; join with sl st to top of ch-3. Break off.

2nd rnd Sl st in any ch-1 sp, ch 3, in same sp work 1 dc, ch 1 and 2 dc (first corner), * ch 1, in next ch-1 sp work 2 dc, ch 1 and 2 dc (another corner). Repeat from * twice more; ch 1; join. Break off.

3rd rnd Sl st in any ch-1 corner sp and work a first corner in same sp, * ch 1, 3-dc shell in next ch-1 sp, ch 1, work corner in next corner sp. Repeat from * twice more; ch 1, shell in next sp, ch 1; join. Break off.

Work first 2 rnds of each square in assorted colors and 3rd rnd always in main color.

To Assemble Hold 2 squares together with right sides facing. With yarn and tapestry needle, whipstitch squares tog, working through 1 lp only of each st (2 small ridges formed by unworked lps on right side). Following assembly diagram, join remaining squares. Join edge A to edge B (see diagram p. 75), forming ring for neck opening.

Collar With right side facing you, using P, work 1 rnd sc evenly around neck opening. Work sc in each sc around until turtleneck measures 3″ from beg; sl st in next sc. Break off.

PUTTING-ON-THE-DOG COAT

Edging With P, work 2 rnds sc evenly around entire outer edge of coat, working 3 sc in each corner. Break off.

Tail-Catcher With P, ch 9. **1st row** Sc in 2nd ch from hook and, in each ch across; ch 1, turn. **2nd row** Sc in each sc across. Break off. Following diagram, sew ends in place.

Sew on buttons. To fasten, slip buttons through sps on corresponding squares.

FLAMBOYANT AFGHAN

Joyous colors tumbling here and there like wild flowers blazing in a summer field make this an afghan to treasure. Ninety-nine grannies in a slightly different combination of double crochet and chains give it an original look.

Size Approximately 64″ x 78″.

Materials About 64 ounces knitting worsted in assorted colors (afghan shown used 30 colors in all—shades of yellow, blue, green, purple, red and brown, as well as white and a little black. Use leftover yarn if desired, purchasing some if necessary to coordinate colors with skeins you may have); aluminum crochet hook size G *or the size that will give you the correct gauge;* tapestry needle.

Gauge 4 dc=1″; each square measures about 7″.

Squares (make 99) There is no particular pattern according to which the colors are changed on the afghan squares. Some squares change colors every rnd and others have 2 or more rnds worked with the same color. If you wish to change colors, simply break off at the end of a rnd and start with a new color as specified under "Changing Colors", p. 140.

Starting at center, ch 6. Join with sl st to form ring.

1st rnd Work 12 sc in ring; join with sl st in back lp of first sc. From now on work in back lp only of each st.

2nd rnd Ch 3, dc in next 2 sc, (ch 5, dc in each of next 3 sc) 3 times; ch 5; join with sl st in top of ch-3.

3rd rnd Ch 3, dc in next 2 dc, dc in next ch, * ch 7, sk 3 ch, dc in next ch, dc in next 3 dc, dc in next ch. Repeat from * twice more; ch 7, sk 3 ch, dc in next ch; join.

4th rnd Ch 3, dc in next 3 dc, * dc in each of next 3 ch, work dc, ch 5 and dc in next ch, dc in each of next 3 ch, dc in next 5 dc. Repeat from * twice more; dc in each of next 3 ch, work dc, ch 5 and dc in next ch, dc in each of next 3 ch, dc in next dc; join (13 dc on each side of square).

5th rnd Ch 3, dc in next 7 dc, * dc in each of next 2 ch, work 3 dc in next ch (corner), dc in each of next 2 ch, dc in next 13 dc. Repeat from * 3 times more, ending last repeat by working 5 dc instead of 13; join (80 dc).

6th rnd Ch 3, dc in next 2 dc, * (ch 1, sk 1 dc, dc in next 2 dc) twice; ch 2, sk 2 dc, work 5 dc in next dc (corner), ch 2, sk 2 dc, dc

in next 2 dc, ch 1, sk 1 dc, dc in next 2 dc, ch 1, sk 1 dc, dc in next 3 dc. Repeat from * 3 times more, ending last repeat by omitting last 3 dc; join. Break off.

To Assemble Hold 2 squares with right sides facing. Whip-stitch them tog along one edge, working through one lp only of each st (ridges formed on right side). Make 11 strips with 9 squares in each strip. Sew strips tog in same manner as for squares.

Border Work dc in each st around, working 5 dc in each corner; join and break off.

ONE-COLOR GRANNY AFGHAN

Even though granny afghans are usually a Joseph's coat of many colors, yours could be made of one soft shade. Squares are interesting variations of double-crochet rounds and cluster rounds, while the scalloped edging is single, double and treble crochet.

Size About 58½" x 75".

Materials Knitting worsted, 40 ounces; crochet hook size H *or the size that will give you the correct gauge.*

Gauge Each square measures 6".

Squares (make 108) Starting at center, ch 5. Join with sl st to form ring.

1st rnd Ch 3, work 11 dc in ring; join with sl st to top of ch-3 (12 dc, counting ch-3 as 1 dc).

2nd rnd Pull up a lp on hook ½" high, y o, insert hook in same st as sl st, y o, draw up a lp, * (y o, insert hook in same st, y o, draw up a lp) twice (7 lps on hook), y o, draw through all lps on hook, ch 1 (cluster made); y o, insert hook in next dc, y o, draw up a lp. * Repeat from * to * 11 times more, omitting "y o, insert hook in next dc, y o, draw up a lp" after last cluster and ending ch 1, sl st to top of first cluster (12 clusters).

3rd rnd Sl st in first sp between clusters, ch 3, dc in same sp (half of corner made), * (1 dc in top of next cluster, 1 dc in next sp) twice; 1 dc in next cluster; work 2 dc, ch 2 and 2 dc in next sp (corner made). Repeat from * twice more; (1 dc in top of next cluster, 1 dc in next sp) twice; 1 dc in next cluster; ending 2 dc in first sp, ch 2, sl st to top of ch-3 (9 dc on each side and 4 corner sps). Now work back and forth in rows.

4th rnd Turn, sl st to center of first sp, draw up a lp ½" high and work a 7-lp cluster in same sp (half of corner made), * (sk 1 dc, 1 cluster in next dc) 4 times; sk 1 dc, work 1 cluster, ch 3 and 1 cluster in next sp. Repeat from * twice more; (sk 1 dc, 1 cluster in next dc) 4 times; ending 1 cluster in first sp, ch 3, sl st to top of first cluster (6 clusters on each side and 4 corner sps).

5th rnd Turn, ch 3, work 1 dc, ch 3 and 2 dc in corner sp, * (2 dc between next 2 clusters) 5 times; work 2 dc, ch 3 and 2 dc in next sp. Repeat from * twice more, ending (2 dc between next 2 clusters) 5 times; sl st to top of ch-3. Break off.

Finishing Afghan is 9 squares wide by 12 squares long. Join as follows: With wrong sides of 2 squares tog, insert hook through both corners, 1 sc in same sp, * ch 1, sk 1 st on both squares, (1 sc through next st on both squares) twice. Repeat from *, ending 1 sc through corner of both squares. Break off.

Scalloped Edge Insert hook in corner, * sk 2 sts, work 3 dc, 3 tr and 3 dc in next st, sk 2 sts, 1 sc in next st. Repeat from * once more, sk 2 sts, work 3 dc, 3 tr and 3 dc in next st, 1 sc in st joining squares. Repeat from * around afghan. Break off.

PETIT SQUARE BEDSPREAD

*Three-round grannies–600 of them–are joined to make this splen-
did spread. (A smaller afghan could be made with just half as
many squares.) Start collecting knitting worsted leftovers from
your friends and you'll soon have enough yarn to make this great
cover.*

Size Approximately 60″ x 90″.

Materials Knitting worsted, nine (4-ounce) skeins main color
(MC), nine (4-ounce) skeins of varied colors of your choice, or
comparable amount of leftover knitting worsted; crochet hook
size F or G *or the size that will give you the correct gauge;* tapestry
needle.

Gauge Each square measures 3″.

NOTE: Afghan as shown is made of 600 squares. Vary colors on
first and second rnds at random, according to your taste. The
third rnd always remains the same (MC).

Squares Starting at center, ch 5 with first color. Join with sl st
to form ring.

1st rnd Ch 3, work 2 dc in ring, (ch 2, 3 dc in ring) 3 times; ch 2,
sl st in 3rd ch of ch-3. Break off.

2nd rnd Join second color in corner ch-2 sp; ch 3, in same sp
work 2 dc, ch 2 and 3 dc (first corner), * ch 1, in next ch-2 sp,
work 3 dc, ch 2 and 3 dc. Repeat from * twice more; ch 1; join.
Break off.

3rd rnd Join MC in corner sp and work a first corner in same
sp, * ch 1, 3 dc in next ch-1 sp, ch 1, work 3 dc, ch 2 and 3 dc in
ch-2 corner sp. Repeat from * twice more; ch 1, 3 dc in next sp,
ch 1; join. Break off.

Finishing Hold 2 squares with right sides facing. Whipstitch
tog along one side. Join squares tog in rows of 20. Join 30 rows
tog to form bedspread.

DREAM-OF-A-BEDSPREAD

Grannies–big and little–make up this dreamy bedcover. Since the combination of colors is so important here, each round of every granny is carefully spelled out in the directions. And just so you won't mix up the squares, you tag each one with a little number. Then it will be a cinch to assemble the spread.

Size 80″ x 120″.

Materials Bear Brand Winsom Orlon acrylic yarn, 31 (2-ounce) skeins black No. 350 (color B), 21 skeins winter white No. 330 (W), 2 skeins green mist No. 361 (G), 1 skein each melon whip No. 359 (salmon, S), brick No. 332 (red-orange, O), evening mist No. 73 (dark gray, D), royal blue No. 292 (R), Pompeii No. 339 (rust, P), rose mist No. 314 (M), autumn mist No. 315 (tan, T); aluminum crochet hook size F *or the size that will give you the correct gauge.*

Gauge Each large square measures 10″; each small square measures 5″.

Squares Starting at center, ch 4. Join with sl st to form ring.

1st rnd Ch 3, work 2 dc in ring, (ch 1, 3-dc shell in ring) 3 times; ch 1; join with sl st to top of ch-3. Break off.

2nd rnd Sl st in any ch-1 sp, ch 3, in same sp work 2 dc, ch 1 and 3 dc (first corner), * ch 1, in next ch-1 sp work 3 dc, ch 1 and 3 dc (another corner). Repeat from * twice more; ch 1; join. Break off.

3rd rnd Sl st in any ch-1 corner sp and work a first corner in same sp, * ch 1, 3-dc shell in next ch-1 sp, ch 1, work corner in next corner sp. Repeat from * twice more; ch 1, shell in next sp, ch 1; join. Break off.

4th rnd Sl st in any ch-1 corner sp and work a first corner in same sp, * (ch 1, shell in next ch-1 sp) twice; ch 1, work corner in next corner sp. Repeat from * twice more; (ch 1, shell in next sp) twice; ch 1; join. Break off.

5th rnd Sl st in any ch-1 corner sp and work a first corner in same sp, * ch 1, work shell in next ch-1 sp. Repeat from * to next corner, ch 1, work a corner in next corner sp. Continue around in pattern; join. Break off.

Repeat last rnd, working 12 rnds for the large squares and 6 rnds for the small squares, in the color sequences given below. All squares are large except for squares No. 6, 9, 21, 25, 45 and 75, which are composed of 4 small squares each.

NOTE: When working consecutive rnds in the same color, see "Changing Colors," page 140. Tag each square upon completion for easier identification when assembling bedspread.

Square 1 2 rnds B, 1 G, 1 O, 2 W, 2 B, 4 W. **Square 2** 2 P, 1 G, 1 W, 2 B, 1 P, 2 W, 3 B. **Square 3** (3 W, 3 B) twice. **Square 4** 2 B, 1 W, 1 B, 2 T, 1 B, 1 W, 2 P, 2 B. **Square 5** 2 G, 2 B, 1 S, 2 B, 3 W, 2 B. **Square 6 (consists of 4 small squares): 1st square** (2 B, 1 W) twice. **2nd square** 2 R, 1 S, 1 B, 1 W, 1 B. **3rd square** 2 P, 1 W, 3 B. **4th square** 1 B , 1 W, 2 B, 2 W.

Square 7 2 B, 1 W, 1 S, (2 B, 2 W) twice. **Square 8** 2 D, 1 G, 2 W, 3 B, 3 W, 1 B. **Square 9 (4 small squares): 1st square** 2 B, 1 W, 1 B, 2 W. **2nd square** 2 R, 1 W, 3 B. **3rd square** 3 G, 1 W, 2 B. **4th square** 2 D, 1 B, 1 W, 2 B.

Square 10 2 R, 1 B, 2 W, 1 B, 3 O, 1 B , 1 W, 1 B. **Square 11** Repeat Square 1. **Square 12** 2 W, 1 B, 1 W, 1 G, (1 W, 1 B) twice; 1 G, 1 W, 1 B. **Square 13** 3 W, 2 G, 4 B, 1 W, 2 B. **Square 14** 2 P, (2 B, 1 W) 3 times; 1 B. **Square 15** 2 O, 1 T, 1 B, 1 W, 2 B, 2 W, 3 B. **Square 16** 5 W, 1 B, 1 W, 3 B, 2 W. **Square 17** 2 G, 1 R, 2 W, 2 B, 1 W, 3 B, 1 W. **Square 18** 2 W, 1 O, 1 B, 1 W, 2 B, 1 W, 1 B, 1 W, 2 B. **Square 19** 2 R, 1 G, 1 B, 1 W , 2 B, 2 W, 3 B. **Square 20** 2 W, 1 B, 1 W , 1 R, 1 B, 1 W, 1 B, 1 T, 1 B, 1 W, 1 B. **Square 21 (4 small squares); 1st square** 2 D, 1 G, 3 B. **2nd square** 2 W, 1 S, 1 B, 1 W, 1 B. **3rd square** 3 B, 2 W, 1 B. **4th square** 3 W, 1 T , 2 B.

Square 22 Repeat Square 4. **Square 23** 2 M, 1 G , 2 W, 3 B, 2 W, 2 B. **Square 24** 3 W, 2 T , 4 B, 1 W, 2 B. **Square 25 (4 small squares): 1st square** 2 W, 2 B, 1 W, 1 B. **2nd square** 2 B, 1 G , 1 W, 2 B. **3rd square** 2 W, 1 B, 1 W, 2 B. **4th square** 2 M, 1 B, 1 W, 2 B.

Square 26 Repeat Square 8. **Square 27** 2 W, 1 P , 1 W, 2 B, 1 W, 1 B, 1 W, 2 T, 1 B. **Square 28** 2 B, 1 W, 1 P, (1 B, 1 W) 3 times; 2 G. **Square 29** Repeat Square 7. **Square 30** 2 W, 1 R , (1 B, 1 W) twice; 2 B, 1 W, 1 B, 1 W. **Square 31** 2 B, 1 D, 1 R, 2 W, 3 B, 1 W, 2 B. **Square 32** 2 M, 1 B, 1 W, 2 B, (1 W, 1 B) 3 times. **Square 33** 2 W, 1 B, 1 G, 1 B, 2 W, 1 B, 2 O, 1 B, 1 W.

Square 34 2 G, 1 B, 2 W, 1 B, 3 R, 1 B, 1 W, 1 B. **Square 35** 2 W, 1 R, 1 S, 1 B, 1 W, 2 B, 1 W, 1 B, 2 W. **Square 36** Repeat Square 14. **Square 37** (2 W, 4 B) twice. **Square 38** Repeat Square 15. **Square 39** 2 B, 1 D, 1 S, 3 B, 2 W, 3 B. **Square 40** 2 B, 1 W, 1 B, 2 W, 1 G, 3 B, 2 W. **Square 41** 2 G, 1 W, 1 B, 1 W, 1 P, 1 B, 1 W, 1 B, 2 W, 1 B. **Square 42** 2 R, 1 M, 1 W, 1 G, 2 B, 2 W, 3 B. **Square 43** Repeat Square 27. **Square 44** 2 R, 2 B, (1 W, 2 B) twice; 1 W, 1 B. **Square 45 (4 small squares): 1st square** 2 G, 1 R, 1 W, 2 B. **2nd square** 2 B, 1 O, 1 B, 1 W, 1 B. **3rd square** 1 B, 1 W, 2 B, 1 W, 1 B. **4th square** 2 B, 1 T, 2 W, 1 B.

Square 46 2 B, 1 W, 2 D, (2 B, 1 W) twice; 1 B. **Square 47** (3 B, 3 W) twice. **Square 48** 2 W, 1 G, 2 B, 1 G, 2 W, 3 B, 1 W. **Square 49** 3 M, 1 B, 1 P, 3 W, 1 B, 1 M, 1 B, 1 W. **Square 50** Repeat Square 33. **Square 51** 2 M, 1 W, 1 M, 2 W, 1 B, 3 D, 1 W, 1 B. **Square 52** 2 W, 2 B, 1 W, 1 M, 3 B, 1 W, 2 B. **Square 53** (1 W, 1 B) twice; 1 W, 1 S, 2 B, 2 W, 2 B. **Square 54** 2 R, 2 B, 1 W, 3 D, 4 B. **Square 55** (1 W, 1 B) twice; 1 W, 1 P, (1 W, 2 B) twice. **Square 56** 2 R, 1 G, 2 W, 3 B, 2 W, 2 B. **Square 57** Repeat Square 41. **Square 58** (3 W, 3 B) twice. **Square 59** 2 S, 1 B, 1 W, 2 B, (1 W, 1 B) 3 times. **Square 60** 2 W, 1 B, 1 W, 2 P, 1 T, 2 B, 2 W, 1 B. **Square 61** 2 T, 1 R, 1 W, 2 B, 1 T, 2 W, 3 B.

Square 62 2 P, 1 W, 2 B, 1 W, 1 R, 1 W, 2 B, 1 W, 1 B. **Square 63** 2 W, 1 P, 2 B, 1 P, 2 W, 3 B, 1 W. **Square 64** Repeat Square 32. **Square 65** 2 B, 1 G, 1 S, 2 W, 2 B, 4 W. **Square 66** 3 W, 2 O, 4 B, 1 W, 2 B. **Square 67** (3 B, 3 W) twice. **Square 68** 2 T, 1 M, 2 W, 3 B, 2 W, 2 B. **Square 69** 2 W, 1 B, 1 W, 1 M, 1 B, 1 W, 2 B, 1 W, 1 B, 1 W. **Square 70** 2 B, 1 D, 1 G, 3 B, 2 W, 3 B. **Square 71** Repeat Square 51. **Square 72** 3 W, 2 S, 4 B, 1 W, 2 B. **Square 73** 2 B, 1 P, 2 W, 2 B, 3 W, 2 B. **Square 74** 2 B, 1 W, 1 B, 2 G, 1 B, 1 W, 2 O, 2 B. **Square 75 (4 small squares): 1st square** 3 R, 1 W, 2 B. **2nd square** (1 W, 1 B) 3 times. **3rd square** 2 T, 1 W, 2 B, 1 W. **4th square** 2 W, 1 R, 2 B, 1 W.

Square 76 2 W, 1 R, 1 B, 1 W, 2 B, 1 W, 1 B, 1 W, 2 B. **Square 77** 2 D, 1 W, 1 D, 2 W, 2 D, 1 B, 3 W.

To Assemble Hold Squares 1 and 2 with right sides facing. Whipstitch them tog along one edge, working through one lp only of each st (2 ridges formed on right side); join Square 3 to Square 2, 4 to 3 and 5 to 4. Join 4 small squares to form Square 6. Join 6 to 5 and 7 to 6, forming a 7-square strip.

Join remaining squares in consecutive order to make 10 more 7-square strips. Sew strips tog to form bedspread.

Border: 1st rnd With B work a first corner (as in granny square) in any corner sp of spread; continue as for 5th rnd of square, working completely around spread. Work 2 more rnds B, 2 rnds W, 5 B, 1 W and 2 B. Break off.

OUT-OF-THE-ORDINARY CRIB AFGHAN

The traditional granny in pastel colors has been a favorite for babies' coverlets for years. Here's an ideal cover but in non-traditional colors – and what terrific colors – bright pink, yellow and purple! The squares combined with supple double-crochet shells make such a great afghan you may want to make a full-size one too.

Size 28" x 41".

Materials Knitting worsted, 7 ounces each bright pink (color A), yellow (B) , purple (C); aluminum crochet hook size F *or the size that will give you the correct gauge.*

Gauge Each square measures 3".

Center-Strip Squares (make 5) Starting at center with A, ch 6. Join with sl st to form ring.

1st rnd Ch 3, work 2 dc in ring, (ch 1, 3-dc shell in ring) 3 times; ch 1; join with sl st to top of ch-3. Break off.

2nd rnd With B sl st in any ch-1 sp, ch 3, in same sp work 2 dc, ch 1 and 3 dc (first corner), * ch 1, in next ch-1 sp work 3 dc, ch 1 and 3 dc (another corner). Repeat from * twice more; ch 1; join.

3rd rnd Sl st to ch-1 corner sp and work a first corner in same sp, * ch 1, 3-dc shell in next ch-1 sp, ch 1, work corner in next corner sp. Repeat from * twice more; ch 1, shell in next sp, ch 1; join. Break off.

Hold 2 squares with right sides facing. Whipstitch tog along one side. Join to the remaining 3 squares in this manner to form one strip.

One-Color Border around Strip: 1st rnd Sl st with C in any corner sp on strip, work a first corner in same sp, * ch 1, work shell in next ch-1 sp. Repeat from * to next corner, also working a shell in each joining between squares. At corner ch 1, work a corner in corner sp. Work completely around strip. Break off. Repeat rnd 6 times more. Break off.

Inner Border of Squares (make 24) Use B for first rnd, C for 2nd rnd, and A for 3rd rnd. Join 2 strips of 7 squares each and 2 strips of 3 squares each. Whipstitch short strips to end of One-Color Border and long strips to sides. Join a square in each corner. Sl st with B in any corner sp and work 1 rnd as for first

rnd of One-Color Border. Break off. Work 5 rnds with A and 1 with B in same manner. Break off.

Outer Border of Squares (make 40) Use B for first rnd, A for 2nd rnd, and C for 3rd rnd. Join 2 strips of 7 squares each and 2 strips of 11 squares each. Whipstitch short strips to ends of afghan and long strips to sides. Add corner squares. Sl st with B in any corner sp and work 2 rnds as for first rnd of One-Color Border. Do not break off.

Edging For picot, ch 4, sc in 4th ch from hook (picot made), sc in each of next 5 sts, * work picot, sc in next 5 sts. Repeat from * around; join. Break off.

RUSTIC PLACE MAT

At last for the inveterate granny maker here's a way to use those little squares in the dining room. This country-look place mat is made of machine-washable cotton. You could use the traditional granny colors, as shown here, or pick up the colors in your china pattern.

Size About 12½" x 17".

Materials For one mat: Coats & Clark's Speed-Cro-Sheen, 2 balls black, 1 ball each mid rose, chartreuse green, parakeet and dark lavender; crochet hook size E *or the size that will give you the correct gauge;* tapestry needle.

Gauge Each square measures 3¼".

Squares (make 20) Starting at center with mid rose, ch 6. Join with sl st to form ring.

1st rnd Ch 3, work 2 dc in ring, (ch 1, 3-dc shell in ring) 3 times; ch 1; join with sl st to top of ch-3. Break off.

2nd rnd With chartreuse green, sl st in any ch-1 sp, ch 3, in same sp work 2 dc, ch 1 and 3 dc (first corner), * ch 1, in next ch-1 sp work 3 dc, ch 1 and 3 dc (another corner). Repeat from * twice more; ch 1; join. Break off.

3rd rnd With parakeet sl st in any ch-1 corner sp and work a first corner in same sp, * ch 1, 3-dc shell in next ch-1 sp, ch 1, work corner in next corner sp. Repeat from * twice more; ch 1, shell in next sp, ch 1; join. Break off.

4th rnd With dark lavender sl st in any ch-1 corner sp and work a first corner in same sp, * (ch 1, shell in next ch-1 sp) twice; ch 1, work corner in next corner sp. Repeat from * twice more; (ch 1, shell in next sp) twice; ch 1; join. Break off.

5th rnd With black sl st in any ch-1 corner sp and work a first corner in same sp, * ch 1, work shell in next ch-1 sp. Repeat from * to next corner, ch 1, work a corner in next corner sp. Continue around in pattern; join. Break off.

To Assemble Hold 2 squares wrong sides tog and whip tog with black, going into only one lp of each stitch along edge. This leaves a little ridge on right side along each side of joining. Make 4 strips of 5 squares each. Join strips.

Border With black sl st in each st around, working 3 sc in each
corner of mat. However, to even out the edges of mat on border
rnd work as follows: Sl st to within 1 st of joining between
squares, sc in next st, h dc in joining, sc in first st of next square.
Break off.

RUGGED HEARTH RUG

Three variations of the granny are used in this sturdy rug that would look as well at a bedside as it does on a stone hearth. The three bold center squares are four times the size of the others. A wide border of blue and red provides a neat frame for the rug.

Size Approximately 38″ x 70″.
Materials Aunt Lydia's heavy rug yarn, 16 (70-yard) skeins medium blue No. 214 (color A), 8 skeins phantom red No. 252 (B), 13 skeins rust No. 227 (C), 9 skeins orange No. 226-A (D); aluminum crochet hook size H *or the size that will give you the correct gauge;* tapestry needle with large eye.
Gauge 8 dc (on border) = 3″; 1 row dc = 1″.
NOTE: Use yarn double throughout.
Large Center Squares (make 3) Each square measures 10″. Using B and starting at center, ch 6. Join with sl st to form ring.
1st rnd Work 2 sc in back lp of each ch around (12 sc). Do not join, but mark the beg of next 2 rnds with a pin. Work in back lp only of each st throughout.
2nd rnd Sc in each sc around, drawing up lp for each sc about ½″ (12 sc).
3rd rnd Work 2 sc in each sc around (24 sc); join with sl st to first sc. Break off.
4th rnd Attach A to any sc, ch 4, sk 2 sc, sc in next sc. Repeat from * 6 times more; ch 4; join with sl st at base of first ch-4.
5th rnd Sl st in next ch-4 lp, work sc, dc and tr in same lp, ch 4, (work sc, dc and tr in next lp, ch 4) 7 times; join with sl st to first sc. Break off.
6th rnd Attach C with sl st in any ch-4 lp, ch 3, work 2 dc, ch 2 and 3 dc in same lp (corner), * ch 1, work 3 dc in next ch-4 lp, ch 1, work 3 dc, ch 2 and 3 dc in next lp (corner). Repeat from * twice more; ch 1, work 3 dc in next lp, ch 1; join to top of ch-3.
7th rnd Ch 3, * dc in each st to corner ch-2 sp, work 2 dc, ch 2 and 2 dc in ch-2 sp (corner). Repeat from * around; dc in each remaining st (60 dc); join. Break off.
8th rnd Attach D. Repeat 7th rnd (76 dc). Break off.
Small Center Squares (make 28) Each square measures 5″. With A, starting at center, ch 6. Join with sl st to form ring.

1st rnd Ch 3, work 2 dc in ring, (ch 2, work 3 dc in ring) 3 times; ch 2; join with sl st to top of ch-3.

2nd rnd Ch 3, 2 dc in same st, (ch 2, work 3 dc in next ch-2 sp, ch 1, 3 dc in next dc) 3 times; ch 2, 3 dc in next sp, ch 1; join.

3rd rnd Sc in top of ch-3; working in back lp only of each st, sc in next 7 sts, * work sc, ch 1 and sc in next ch-1 sp (corner), sc in next 8 sts. Repeat from * twice more; work corner in last sp; join (40 sc). Break off.

Border Squares (make 32) Each square measures 5″. With B, starting at center, ch 2. Work 4 sc in 2nd ch from hook. Do not join.

1st rnd Work 2 sc in each sc around (8 sc); join with sl st in first sc.

2nd rnd Work in back lp only of each st. Ch 3, dc in next sc (first point of star made), * ch 2, y o, draw up lp in same sc, y o, draw through 2 lps on hook, y o, draw up lp in next sc, y o, draw through 2 lps on hook, y o, draw through all 3 lps on hook (another point of star made). Repeat from * 6 times more; ch 2; join with sl st to top of ch-3. Break off.

3rd rnd With C sl st in any ch-2 sp, ch 3, work 2 dc in same sp, ch 1, in next sp work 2 dc, tr, ch 2, tr and 2 dc (corner), * ch 1, work 3 dc in next sp, ch 1; make a corner in next sp. Repeat from * twice more; ch 1; join. Break off.

Block each square carefully to measurement.

Joining For all joinings, hold squares tog with right sides facing. Whipstitch through 1 lp only of each st so that free lps form ridge on right side. Whipstitch two Small Center Squares tog. Sew 9 more pairs of these squares in same manner. Hold a pair along one side of a Large Center Square and join, pulling slightly to fit if necessary. Sew pairs of squares along remaining 3 sides. Sew pairs of squares in same manner around only 3 sides of other two Center Squares. Following photograph, whipstitch the 3 large squares tog to form center panel. Fill in corners and spaces along sides with remaining Small Center Squares.

Inner Double Crochet Border Work in back lp only of each st. With D, sl st in a corner sp of center panel, ch 3, work dc, ch 1 and 2 dc in same sp, dc in each st around, working 2 dc, ch 1 and 2 dc in each corner sp; join with sl st in top of ch-3. Break off.

Join 2 strips of 6 Border Squares each for rug ends and 2 strips of 10 squares each for sides. Sew strips in place, pulling slightly to fit if necessary.

Outer Border 1st rnd With D, sl st in a corner sp, ch 3, work dc, ch 1 and 2 dc in same sp, dc around rug, keeping edges smooth and flat, and work 2 dc, ch 1 and 2 dc in each corner ch-2 sp; join. Break off.

2nd rnd With A, sl st in a corner ch-1 sp and work 2 sc, ch 1 and 2 sc in same sp (corner), sc in each st around, working a corner in each corner sp; join. Break off.

3rd rnd With B, repeat last rnd. Break off.

4th rnd With D, work as for last rnd, working dcs instead of scs. Break off.

Picot Edging With D, sl st in a corner and work across narrow end of rug as follows: Work sc in same st, for picot ch 3, sc in 3rd ch from hook (picot made), * sc in each of next 5 sts, work picot. Repeat from * across end of rug, sc in last st. Break off. Repeat across opposite end of rug.

HAIL TO THE HASSOCK

Slipcover a hassock with five great granny squares that start with a big round. Neat border is single crochet. This sturdy cover fits a fourteen-inch hassock. If yours is larger, just add more rows of single crochet.

Size Fits a 14″ hassock.

Materials Fleisher's Gigantic (bulky yarn), 1 (2-ounce) skein orange spice No. 759 (color A), 2 skeins antique gold No. 753 (B), 5 skeins pistachio No. 777 (C), 6 skeins forest green No. 446 (D); aluminum crochet hook size H *or the size that will give you the correct gauge.*

Gauge 3 sc on border =1″. Squares measure about 14½″.

Squares (make 5) Use color A through 2nd rnd, color B for 3rd and 4th rnds, color C for 5th, 6th and 7th rnds.

Starting at center, ch 6. Join with sl st to form ring.

1st rnd Ch 3, work 15 dc in ring; join with sl st to top of ch-3 (16 dc, counting ch-3 as 1 dc).

2nd rnd Ch 4, dc in next dc, * ch 1, dc in next dc. Repeat from * around, ending with ch 1; join with sl st in 3rd ch of ch-4. Break off.

3rd rnd Sl st in any ch-1 sp, ch 3, work 2 dc in same sp, * ch 1, 3 dc in next sp. Repeat from * around, ending with ch 1; join (48 dc, counting ch-3 as 1 dc).

4th rnd Ch 3, dc in each of next 2 dc, * ch 1, dc in each of next 3 dc. Repeat from * around, ending with ch 1; join. Break off.

5th rnd Sl st in any ch-1 sp, ch 8, dc in next ch-1 sp (first corner lp), * (ch 3, dc in next ch-1 sp) 3 times; ch 5, dc in next ch-1 sp (another corner lp). Repeat from * twice more; (ch 3, dc in next sp) twice; ch 3; join with sl st in 3rd ch of ch-8.

6th rnd Sl st in next corner lp, ch 3, in same lp work 2 dc, ch 3 and 3 dc, * (ch 1, work 3 dc in next ch-3 sp) 3 times; ch 1, work 3 dc, ch 3 and 3 dc in next corner lp. Repeat from * twice more; (ch 1, 3 dc in next sp) 3 times; ch 1; join.

7th rnd Sl st in each st to corner ch-3 sp, sl st in same sp, ch 3, in same sp work 2 dc, ch 3 and 3 dc, * (ch 1, dc in each of next 3 dc) 5 times; ch 1, work 3 dc, ch 3 and 3 dc in next corner sp. Repeat from * twice more; (ch 1, dc in each of next 3 dc) 5 times; ch 1; join. Break off.

Border Work in back lp only of each st for all remaining rnds.

1st rnd Sl st with D in any corner ch-1 sp, * work sc, ch 1 and sc in same sp (corner), work sc in each dc and ch st around, working corner in each ch-3 corner sp; join with sl st in first sc.

2nd rnd Sc in next sc, work corner in ch-1 sp, sc in each sc around, working corner in each ch-1 corner sp; join. Repeat 2nd rnd twice more. Break off.

To Assemble Hold 2 squares with wrong sides facing. With D, working through both lps on each square, sc along one side to join. Make a strip of 4 squares, then join to form tube. Join remaining square to one end of tube to form top of hassock.

PRETTY PILLOW

You never can have too many squashy toss pillows, and this pretty one will fit into any collection. Fifteen inches square, it's just one big granny on a felt back. Made of bulky yarns, it's a smashing combination of brick, reds and pink.

Size 15″ square.

Materials Brunswick Aspen (bulky yarn), 1 (2-ounce) skein each brick heather No. 1474 (color A), ginger heather No. 14861 (B), cotton candy No. 14581 (C), cherry smash No. 1420 (D); aluminum crochet hook size H; ½ yard orange felt; 1 pound kapok or Dacron for stuffing.

Square Starting at center with A, ch 4. Join with sl st to form ring.

1st rnd Ch 2, work 7 h dc in ring (8 h dc, counting ch-2 as 1 h dc); join with sl st to top of ch-2.

2nd rnd Ch 3, work dc in next h dc, * ch 2, y o hook, draw up lp in same st where last dc was made, y o, draw through 2 lps on hook (2 lps remain on hook), y o, draw up lp in next st, y o, draw through 2 lps on hook, y o, draw through remaining 3 lps on hook (dc cl completed). Repeat from * 6 times more; ending last repeat with ch 2, dc in base of ch-3; join with sl st to top of ch-3 (8 dc cl, counting ch-3 as 1 dc). Break off.

3rd rnd With B sl st in any ch-2 sp, ch 3, 2 dc in same sp, * ch 2, 3 dc in next ch-2 sp. Repeat from * around, ending with ch 2; join with sl st to top of ch-3. Do not break off.

4th rnd Sl st in each st to next ch-3 sp, sl st in sp, ch 3, work 3 dc in same sp, * ch 2, 4 dc in next ch-2 sp. Repeat from * around, ending with ch 2; join. Break off.

5th rnd With C sl st in any ch-2 sp, ch 3, in same sp work 3 dc, ch 1 and 4 dc (first corner) , * ch 1, 4 dc shell in next ch-2 sp, ch 1, in next sp work 4 dc, ch 1 and 4 dc (another corner). Repeat from * twice more; ch 1, shell in next ch-2 sp, ch 1; join. Do not break off.

6th rnd Sl st in each st to next corner ch-1 sp, sl st in sp, ch 6, h dc in same sp (first corner lp), * (ch 4, h dc in next ch-1 sp) twice; ch 4, in next ch-1 corner sp work h dc, ch 4 and h dc (another corner lp). Repeat from * twice more; (ch 4, h dc in next ch-1 sp) twice; ch 4; join to 2nd ch of ch-6. Do not break off.

7th rnd Sl st in next corner lp, ch 3, in same lp work 3 dc, ch 1 and 4 dc, * (ch 1, work 4 dc in next ch-4 sp) 3 times; ch 1, work 4 dc, ch 1 and 4 dc in next corner lp. Repeat from * twice more; (ch 1, 4 dc in next ch-4 sp) 3 times; ch 1; join. Break off.

8th rnd With B working in back lp only of each st, sl st in any corner ch-1 st, work sc, ch 1 and sc in same st, sc in each st around, working sc, ch 1 and sc in each corner st; join. Break off.

9th rnd With D sl st in any corner ch-1 sp, ch 3, in same sp work 3 dc, ch 1 and 4 dc, * ch 1, sk next 5 sc, working in back lp only (work 4 dc in next sc, ch 1, sk next 4 sc) 3 times; work 4 dc in next sc, ch 1, sk next 5 sc, work 4 dc, ch 1 and 4 dc in next ch-1 corner sp. Repeat from * twice more; ch 1, sk next 5 sc, (work 4 dc in next sc, ch 1, sk next 4 sc) 3 times; work 4 dc in next sc, ch 1, sk last 5 sc; join. Do not break off.

10th rnd Sl st in each st to next corner ch-1 sp, ch 6, h d c in same sp, * (ch 4, h dc in next ch-1 sp) 5 times; ch 4, h dc in next ch-1 corner sp, ch 4, h dc in same sp. Repeat from * twice more; (ch 4, h dc in next ch-1 sp) 5 times; ch 4; join with sl st in 2nd ch of ch-6. Do not break off.

11th rnd Sl st in next corner lp, ch 3, in same lp work 3 dc, ch 1 and 4 dc, * (ch 1, work 4 dc in next ch-4 sp) 6 times; ch 1, work 4 dc, ch 1 and 4 dc in next corner lp. Repeat from * twice more; (ch 1, 4 dc in next ch-4 sp) 6 times; ch 1; join. Break off.

12th rnd Working in back lp only of each st, using A, sl st in any corner ch-1 sp, work 3 sc in same sp; sc in each st around, working 3 sc in each corner sp; join with sl st in first sc.

13th rnd Working in back lp only of each st, work 3 sc in next (corner) sc; sc in each sc around, working 3 sc in each corner sc; join.

14th and 15th rnds Repeat 13th rnd. Break off.

Finishing Cut two 16" squares felt (½" seam allowance included). Pin or baste granny square on one felt piece, having yarn edge just over seam line. With right sides of felt pieces facing and granny square sandwiched between, stitch around 3 sides, catching yarn edge in stitching. Turn and stuff. Sew fourth side closed.

BIG BOLD FLOOR SHOW

Here's a soft answer to sitting on the floor – a mammoth granny square mounted on a felt pillow. Once you start working on a square, it's hard to stop; this one continues for twenty-six colorful rounds.

Size 29″ square.

Materials Knitting worsted, 2 ounces each orange (color A), yellow (B), purple (C), pink (D), red (E) and navy (F); 1 yard 72″-wide orange felt; five 1-pound bags kapok or ten ½-pound bags Dacron stuffing; aluminum crochet hook size G *or the size that will give you the correct gauge.*

Gauge Shell, ch 1 and shell=1¾″.

Square Start with A. Work 2nd rnd with B, 3rd rnd C, 4th rnd D and 5th rnd B. At end of 5th rnd piece should measure about 5½″ square. Repeat 5th rnd 21 times more, working 1 rnd each E, F, A, D, C, B,F, E and A, then 2 rnds each D, B, C, E, A and F. Break off.

    Starting at center, ch 6. Join with sl st to form ring.

1st rnd Ch 3, work 2 dc in ring, (ch 1, 3-dc shell in ring) 3 times; ch 1; join with sl st to top of ch-3. Break off.

2nd rnd Sl st in any ch-1 sp, ch 3, in same sp work 2 dc, ch 1 and 3 dc (first corner), * ch 1, in next ch-1 sp work 3 dc, ch 1 and 3 dc (another corner). Repeat from * twice more; ch 1; join. Break off.

3rd rnd Sl st in any ch-1 corner sp and work a first corner in same sp, * ch 1, 3-dc shell in next ch-1 sp, ch 1, work corner in next corner sp. Repeat from * twice more; ch 1, shell in next sp, ch 1; join. Break off.

4th rnd Sl st in any ch-1 corner sp and work a first corner in same sp, * (ch 1, shell in next ch-1 sp) twice; ch 1, work corner in next corner sp. Repeat from * twice more; (ch 1, shell in next sp) twice; ch 1; join. Break off.

5th rnd Sl st in any ch-1 corner sp and work a first corner in same sp, * ch 1, work shell in next ch-1 sp. Repeat from * to next corner, ch 1, work a corner in next corner sp. Continue around in pattern; join. Break off.

Pillow Cut two 30″ felt squares (½″ seam allowance included). Pin or baste granny square on one felt piece, having yarn edge

just over seam line. With right sides of felt pieces facing and granny square sandwiched between, stitch around 3 sides, catching yarn edge in stitching. Leave 16″ open on 1 side. Turn and stuff; sew opening.

MULTICOLOR PILLOW

A little edging extends beyond this pillow and dresses up the four-square design. Double yarn used on the first round of each granny makes a puffy little center. To show these squares to the best advantage they are mounted on the pillow wrong side up.

Size Pillow measures 12″ square.

Materials Kentucky All Purpose (rayon) Yarn, 1 (100-yard) skein each dusty rose No. 729, peach No. 707, orange No. 708, deep rose No. 734 and purple No. 714; aluminum crochet hook size E *or the size that will give you the correct gauge;* ½ yard each 36″-wide muslin and natural colored linen; polyester stuffing; 12″ zipper (optional).

Gauge Each square measures 6″.

Squares (make 4) Starting at center, with dusty rose used double, ch 6. Join with sl st to form ring.

1st rnd Ch 3, work 2 dc in ring, (ch 1, 3-dc shell in ring) 3 times; ch 1; join with sl st to top of ch-3. Break off.

2nd rnd With peach, sl st in any ch-1 sp, ch 3, in same sp work 2 dc, ch 1 and 3 dc (first corner), * ch 1, in next ch 1 sp work 3 dc, ch 1 and 3 dc (another corner). Repeat from * twice more; ch 1; join. Break off.

3rd rnd With orange, sl st in any ch-1 corner sp and work a first corner in same sp, * ch 1, 3-dc shell in next ch-1 sp, ch 1, work corner in next corner sp. Repeat from * twice more; ch 1, shell in next sp, ch 1; join. Break off.

4th rnd With deep rose, sl st in any ch-1 corner sp and work a first corner in same sp, * (ch 1, shell in next ch-1 sp) twice; ch 1, work corner in next corner sp. Repeat from * twice more; (ch 1, shell in next sp) twice; ch 1; join. Break off.

5th rnd With purple, sl st in any ch-1 corner sp and work a first corner in same sp, * ch 1, work shell in next ch-1 sp. Repeat from * to next corner, ch 1, work a corner in next corner sp. Continue around in pattern; join. Break off.

Joining Hold 2 squares with wrong sides facing. Whipstitch them tog along one edge for 1 strip. Join 3rd and 4th squares for 2nd strip. Join strips to form large square.

Edging 1st rnd With right side facing you, using deep rose, sc in each st around, working 3 sc in each corner; join. Break off.

2nd rnd With wrong side facing you make lp on hook with orange, y o, * in next sc on last rnd work dc, ch 3 and dc, sk next sc. Repeat from * around; join. Break off.

To Make Pillow Cut two 13″ squares each muslin and linen. Stitch muslin squares tog with ½″ seams, leaving opening for stuffing. Turn and stuff; sew opening.

Seam 3 sides of linen squares; turn. Add zipper if you are using one. Insert pillow. Close zipper or sew remaining side.

Center and pin crocheted piece *wrong* side up on pillow (the first rnd puffs up slightly on wrong side of each square to give it texture). Blindstitch around edges of last sc rnd with matching color thread, so that edging extends beyond pillow.

All About Granny Squares

TO BEGIN CROCHET

When you were about eight years old you probably took a string and made a chain of loops that you pulled through with your fingers. If you did, you know how to crochet, since crochet is essentially a series of loops pulled through with the aid of a hook. A little practice will give you the basic know-how to make granny squares.

CROCHET HOOKS

Crochet hooks come in a wide range of sizes and lengths and are made of a number of materials.

Aluminum and plastic hooks, used for wool yarn and cotton thread, are sized in varying ways by different manufacturers. Some size them by letter, some by number and others by both letter and number. Aluminum and plastic hooks usually come in sizes B through K, size B being the smallest. They may also be numbered in sizes 1 through 10½, size 1 being the smallest.

Steel hooks come in sizes 00, the largest, and 1 to 14, 14 being the smallest.

Bone hooks are generally used for wool yarn and come in sizes 1 (the smallest) through 6 (the largest).

GAUGE

Gauge means the number of stitches to 1" and the number of rows to 1". It is most important that you crochet to the gauge specified so that your finished article will be the correct size.

Make a practice piece at least 2" square, using the hook and materials specified in the directions. With a ruler, measure the number of stitches you have to 1", as in Diagram 1. If your stitches do not correspond in number to the gauge given, experiment with a hook of a different size. If you have more stitches than specified to the inch, you should use a larger hook. If you have fewer stitches to the inch, use a smaller hook.

Keep changing the hook size until your gauge is exactly the same as that specified.

In the case of granny squares, the gauge is generally given for the size of the finished square.

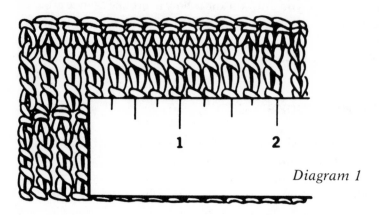

Diagram 1

CROCHET ABBREVIATIONS AND TERMS

Here are the common abbreviations and an explanation of the terms and symbols most frequently used in crochet.

beg .... beginning
bl .... block
ch .... chain
cl .... cluster
dc .... double crochet
dec .... decrease
h dc... half double crochet
inc .... increase
incl .... inclusive
lp .... loop
rnd .... round
sc .... single crochet
sk .... skip
sl .... slip
sl st .... slip stitch
sp .... space
st .... stitch

sts .... stitches
tog .... together
tr .... treble
y o .... yarn over hook

* **Asterisk** means repeat the instructions following the asterisk as many times as specified, in addition to the first time.

[ ] **Brackets** are used to designate changes in size when directions are given, as they often are, for more than one size. The figure preceding the brackets refers to the smallest size.

Even: When directions say "work even," this means to continue working without increasing or decreasing.

Multiple of Stitches: A pattern often requires an exact number of stitches to be worked correctly. When directions say "multiple of" a certain number, it means the number of stitches must be divisible by this number. For example: "multiple of 6" would be 12, 18, 24, etc.; "multiple of 6 plus 3" would be 15, 21, 27, etc.

( ) **Parentheses** mean repeat instructions in parentheses as many times as specified. For example: "(ch 5, sc in next sc) 5 times" means to work all instructions within parentheses 5 times in all.

PRELIMINARY STEPS

Make a practice piece of each new stitch and work until you are familiar with it. To practice, use knitting worsted and an aluminum crochet hook size G.

THE FIRST LOOP

1. Make a loop at the end of yarn and hold loop in place with thumb and forefinger of left hand (Diagram 2: at left is short end of thread; at right is the long, or working, thread).

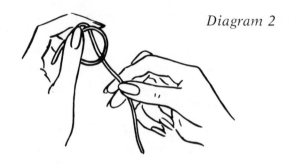

Diagram 2

2. With right hand grasp the crochet hook as you would a pencil and put hook through loop, catch working yarn and draw it through (Diagram 3).

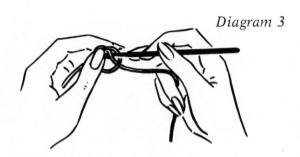

Diagram 3

3. Pull short end and working yarn in opposite directions to bring loop close around the end of hook (Diagram 4).

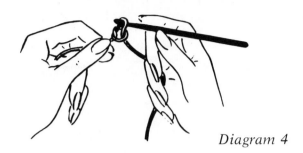

Diagram 4

TO HOLD YARN

1. Measure down working yarn about 4" from loop on hook.

2. At this point insert yarn between ring finger and little finger of left hand (Diagram 5).

Diagram 5

3. Weave yarn toward back, under little and ring fingers, over middle finger and under forefinger, then toward you (Diagram 6).

Diagram 6

4. Grasp hook and loop with thumb and forefinger of left hand. Gently pull working yarn so that it is taut but not tight (Diagram 7).

Diagram 7

TO HOLD HOOK

Hold hook in right hand as you would a pencil, but bring middle finger forward to rest near tip of hook (Diagram 8).

Diagram 8

In order to begin working, adjust fingers of left hand as in Diagram 9. The middle finger is bent so it can control the tension, while the ring and little fingers prevent the yarn from moving too freely. As you practice you will become familiar with the correct tension. Now you are ready to begin the chain stitch.

Diagram 9

CHAIN STITCH (ch)

1. Pass hook under yarn and catch yarn with hook. This is called yarn over—y o (Diagram 10).

Diagram 10

2. Draw yarn through loop on hook. This makes one chain (Diagram 11).

Diagram 11

3. Repeat steps 1 and 2 until you have as many chain stitches as you need. One loop always remains on hook. Keep thumb and forefinger of your left hand near stitch on which you are working. Practice making chains until they are uniform (Diagram 12).

Diagram 12

THE BASIC STITCHES

SINGLE CROCHET (sc)

Make a foundation chain of 20 stitches for practice piece.

1. Insert hook from the front under 2 top threads of 2nd chain from hook (Diagram 13).

2. Yarn over hook (Diagram 14).

3. Draw through stitch. There are now 2 loops on hook (Diagram 15).

Diagram 13

Diagram 14

Diagram 15

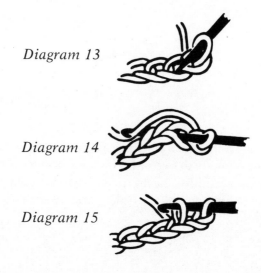

4. Yarn over (Diagram 16). Draw through 2 loops on hook. One loop remains on hook. One single crochet is now completed (Diagram 17).

5. For next single crochet, insert hook under 2 top strands of next stitch (Diagram 18). Repeat steps 2, 3 and 4. Repeat until you have made a single crochet in each chain.

6. At end of row of single crochet, chain 1 (Diagram 19).

7. Turn work so that reverse side is facing you (Diagram 20).

8. Insert hook under 2 top strands of first single crochet. Repeat steps 2, 3, 4, 5, 6 and 7. Continue working single crochet in

this manner until work is uniform and you feel familiar with the stitch. On last row do not make a turning chain. Clip yarn about 3″ from work, bring loose end through the one remaining loop on hook and pull tight (Diagram 21).

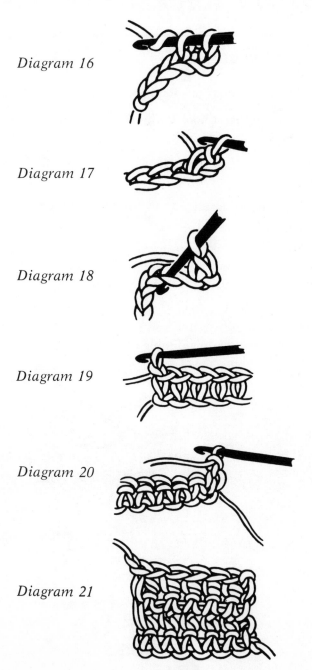

Diagram 16

Diagram 17

Diagram 18

Diagram 19

Diagram 20

Diagram 21

Now you have completed your practice piece of single crochet.

NOTE: In all crochet, pick up the 2 top strands of every stitch unless otherwise directed. When only one strand is picked up, a different effect is produced.

DOUBLE CROCHET (dc)

Make a foundation chain of 20 stitches for practice piece.

1. Yarn over, insert hook under the 2 top strands of 4th chain from hook (Diagram 22).

2. Yarn over, draw through stitch. There are now 3 loops on hook.

3. Yarn over (Diagram 23). Draw through 2 loops. Two loops remain on hook.

4. Yarn over again (Diagram 24). Draw through the 2 remaining loops. One loop remains on hook. One double crochet is now completed (Diagram 25).

5. For next double crochet, yarn over, insert hook under the 2 top strands of next stitch and repeat steps 2, 3 and 4. Repeat until you have made a double crochet in each stitch.

Diagram 22

Diagram 23

Diagram 24

Diagram 25

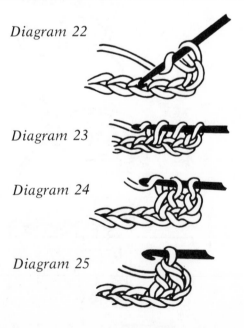

6. At end of row, chain 3 and turn work (Diagram 26).

7. On next row, yarn over, skip first double crochet, insert hook under the 2 top strands of 2nd double crochet.
     Repeat steps 2, 3, 4, 5, 6 and 7 (Diagram 27).

8. Continue working double crochet in this manner until work is uniform and you feel familiar with the stitch. On last row, do not make a turning chain. Clip yarn about 3″ from work, bring loose end through the one remaining loop on hook and pull tight.

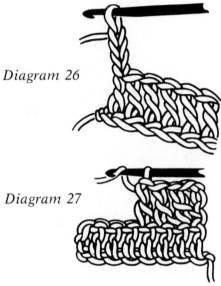

Diagram 26

Diagram 27

HALF DOUBLE CROCHET (h dc)

To make half double crochet, repeat steps 1 and 2 under "Double Crochet" but insert hook in 3rd chain from hook. At this point there are 3 loops on hook. Then yarn over and draw through all 3 loops at once (Diagram 28). Half double crochet is now completed. At end of row, chain 2 to turn.

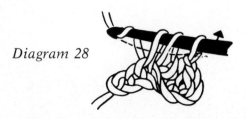

Diagram 28

TREBLE CROCHET (tr)

Make a foundation chain of 20 stitches for practice piece.

1. Yarn over twice, insert hook under 2 top strands of 5th chain from hook.

2. Yarn over and draw a loop through the chain. There are now 4 loops on hook.

3. Yarn over again (Diagram 29). Draw through 2 loops on hook (3 loops remain on hook).

Diagram 29

4. Yarn over again (Diagram 30). Draw through 2 loops (2 loops remain on hook).

5. Yarn over again (Diagram 31). Draw through 2 remaining loops (one loop remains on hook). One treble crochet is now completed. At end of row, chain 4 to turn. Continue making treble crochet in this manner until you are familiar with the stitch. Finish piece in the same way as other pieces.

Diagram 30

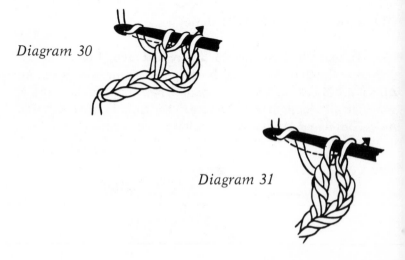

Diagram 31

THE BASIC TECHNIQUES

TO TURN WORK

You will notice that stitches vary in length. Each uses a different number of chain stitches to turn at the end of a row. Below is a table showing the number of chain stitches required to make a turn for each stitch.

Single crochet (sc)...Ch 1 to turn
Half double crochet (h dc)..Ch 2 to turn
Double crochet (dc)..Ch 3 to turn
Treble crochet (tr)..Ch 4 to turn

TO DECREASE (dec) SINGLE CROCHET

1. Work one single crochet to point where 2 loops are on hook. Draw up a loop in next stitch (Diagram 32).

2. Yarn over, draw thread through 3 loops at one time. One decrease made (Diagram 33).

Diagram 32

Diagram 33

TO DECREASE (dec) DOUBLE CROCHET

1. Work one double crochet to point where 2 loops are on hook. Begin another double crochet in next stitch and work until 4 loops are on hook (Diagram 34).

2. Yarn over, draw through 2 loops (Diagram 35).

3. Yarn over, draw through 3 loops (Diagram 36). One decrease made.

Diagram 34

Diagram 35

Diagram 36

TO INCREASE (inc)

When directions call for an increase, work 2 stitches in one stitch. This forms one extra stitch.

SLIP STITCH (sl st)

Make a foundation chain of 20 stitches for practice piece.

Insert hook under top strand of 2nd chain from hook, yarn over. With one motion draw through stitch and loop on hook. Insert hook under top strand of next chain, then yarn over and draw through stitch and loop on hook (Diagram 37).

Repeat until you have made a slip stitch in each chain.

A chain with slip stitch is often used for ties on bonnets, sacques, and other articles that need to be closed without buttons or snaps. Rows of slip stitch worked in the back loop of each stitch produce a ribbed effect.

Diagram 37

SLIP STITCH FOR JOINING

When directions say "join," always use a slip stitch.

1. Insert hook through the 2 top strands of stitch (Diagram 38).

2. Yarn over and with one motion draw through stitch and loop on hook (Diagram 39).

Diagram 38   *Diagram 39*

FINISHING—FASTENING ENDS

After you have completed an article, thread each loose end of thread or yarn in a needle and darn it through a solid part of the crochet to fasten it securely. Cut off remaining yarn close to the work. Be sure starting ends are long enough to be fastened off in this way when article is finished.

HOW TO MAKE GRANNY SQUARES

Let's assume you know how to crochet. If you don't, turn to pages 109-123, where you will find all the help you need to learn the basic techniques.

WHAT IS A GRANNY SQUARE?

It's not easy talking about something we haven't really had in our hands, so let's be specific. A granny is a unit of crochet traditionally composed of only two stitches—chain and double crochet. It always starts at the center with chain stitches slip-stitched into a ring. Then it grows, round by round, combining groups of double-crochet stitches, which form shells, with chain stitches to separate the shells and make the corners.

The traditional granny square is made of five such rounds and ends up, of course, a square. But nowadays one can make as many or as few rounds as one likes, and one can vary the way one combines chains and double crochets. One can, indeed, add or substitute other stitches. One can even turn the old granny square into a rectangle, a triangle, or a five-, six- or eight-sided unit.

TRADITIONAL GRANNY SQUARE

To begin a traditional granny square have ready a small quantity of yarn in five different colors and a crochet hook. Work in rounds from the center out, breaking off the old color and adding the new for each round. Nothing could be easier. But to keep from having all those loose ends to weave in later, try crocheting over the tails as you work.

You could practice with knitting worsted and an aluminum crochet hook size G, but you might like to be able to use your practice squares. In heavy yarn they make excellent potholders (see page 126).

Starting at center, ch 6. Join with sl st to form ring (Diagram 1).

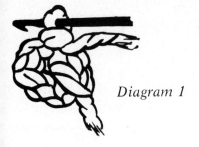

Diagram 1

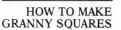

another corner

first corner

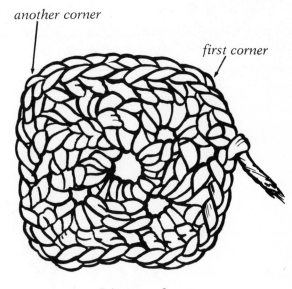

Diagram 3

sl st joining

ch-1

3-dc shell

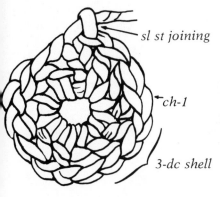

Diagram 2

1st rnd Ch 3, work 2 dc in ring, (ch 1, 3-dc shell in ring) 3 times; ch 1; join with sl st to top of ch-3 (Diagram 2). Break off.

2nd rnd Sl st in any ch-1 sp, ch 3, in same sp work 2 dc, ch 1 and 3 dc (first corner), * ch 1, in next ch-1 sp work 3 dc, ch 1 and 3 dc (another corner). Repeat from * twice more; ch 1; join (Diagram 3). Break off.

3rd rnd Sl st in any ch-1 corner sp and work a first corner in same sp, * ch 1, 3-dc shell in next ch-1 sp, ch 1, work corner in next corner sp. Repeat from * twice more; ch 1, shell in next sp, ch 1; join. Break off.

4th rnd Sl st in any ch-1 corner sp and work a first corner in same sp, * (ch 1, shell in next ch-1 sp) twice; ch 1, work corner in next corner sp. Repeat from * twice more; (ch 1, shell in next sp) twice; ch 1; join. Break off.

5th rnd Sl st in any ch-1 corner sp and work a first corner in same sp, * ch 1, work shell in next ch-1 sp. Repeat from * to next corner, ch 1, work a corner in next corner sp. Continue around in pattern; join. Break off.

GRANNY SQUARE POTHOLDER

For all you tyro crocheters here's the ideal way to learn how to make granny squares. Even though this may be your very first square, you'll still come up with a practical potholder.

Size 6½" square.

Materials Coats & Clark's rug yarn, 1 skein each rose, crystal green, blue, yellow and black; aluminum crochet hook size J *or the size that will give you the correct gauge.*

Gauge Square measures 6½".

Square Starting at center with rose, ch 6. Join with sl st to form ring.

1st rnd Ch 3, work 2 dc in ring, (ch 1, 3-dc shell in ring) 3 times; ch 1; join with sl st to top of ch-3. Break off.

2nd rnd With green sl st in any ch-1 sp, ch 3, in same sp work 2 dc, ch 1 and 3 dc (first corner), * ch 1, in next ch-1 sp work 3 dc, ch 1 and 3 dc (another corner). Repeat from * twice more; ch 1; join. Break off.

3rd rnd With blue sl st in any ch-1 corner sp and work a first corner in same sp, * ch 1, 3-dc shell in next ch-1 sp, ch 1, work corner in next corner sp. Repeat from * twice more; ch 1, shell in next sp, ch 1; join. Break off.

4th rnd With yellow sl st in any ch-1 corner sp and work a first corner in same sp, * (ch 1, shell in next ch-1 sp) twice; ch 1, work corner in next corner sp. Repeat from * twice more; (ch 1, shell in next sp) twice; ch 1; join. Break off.

5th rnd With black sl st in any ch-1 corner sp and work a first corner in same sp, * ch 1, work shell in next ch-1 sp. Repeat from * to next corner, ch 1, work a corner in next corner sp. Continue around in pattern; join. Do not break off.

Hanging Loop Sl st in each st to corner sp, sl st in corner sp, ch 7, sl st in same corner sp. Break off. Weave in end.

YARNS AND COLORS

YARNS

Consider anything you can wrap around a hook as a candidate for a project. Although granny squares were traditionally made of leftover yarns, you can start with a choice of colors, fibers, weights and types of yarn.

An afghan is usually made of yarn of knitting-worsted weight. There is no reason, however, why the worsted can't be combined with other yarns—perhaps a bit of mohair, so that each square has a fluffy center. The knitting worsted can be all wool, so that your afghan is really warm. Or if you use worsted weight of a synthetic fiber such as nylon, Orlon or polyester, it may have the advantage of being machine washable.

Try summer yarn such as Brunswick's Coolspun, a blend of linen and Orlon, used in the belt on page 65. Or Lily Mills' Sugar-'n-Cream cotton yarn. Sport yarn is a great weight for sweaters and vests. Even combine a sport yarn (of a synthetic fiber) with crochet cotton. There are some shiny rayon yarns that will make a fine contrast with the matte look of the wool yarns.

It might be worth your while to buy a skein or ball of an unusual yarn to experiment with before you invest in the full amount you need for a large project. In fact, it's an excellent way to judge how much you will actually need to buy. If you would like to use a yarn such as mohair or angora but find the cost prohibitive, use an expensive yarn for only one round of each granny and a less costly one for the other rounds.

Common hardware-store string is a with-it inexpensive way to work granny square projects. How about a sturdy tote of jute twine? The variety-store counterpart of cotton string— Coats & Clark's Speed-Cro-Sheen—is certainly worth your attention.

Perhaps you have some rattail left over from a macramé project, or you may have other novelty material, such as soutache braid or chenille. Try out various sizes of crochet hooks and you may come up with a totally new crochet yarn. Metallic yarn used alone or in combination with knitting worsted could make a smashing evening jacket.

And don't forget rug yarn. Use it not only in a rug (page 93) but try it for a potholder (page 126) or a hat (page 43). At the other end of the scale are the delicate crewel and tapestry yarns. Used in one or more strands, they offer a wonderful color range that should stimulate all sorts of ideas.

COLORS

As you concoct new yarn combinations, coordinate your ideas with color experiments. A classic granny square module can take on a whole variety of appearances simply through the placement of color (see Drawing 1). The actual crocheting is the same in every unit but the arrangement of colors changes the appearance of each square.

Drawing 1

People seeing a granny project for the first time might think it a haphazard jumble of colors. Nothing could be further from the truth. One should always weigh and balance one color against another. Will the dark red offset the light yellow in the center? Does the square need some green in the last round? Assembling a group of multicolor squares also takes a good eye to balance the light squares against the darks, the pastels against the brights.

If you are planning an afghan for a particular room or a sweater for a particular outfit, you may want to pick up one of the colors in the room or outfit. You might always use one color in the center of every square and then use other colors hit-or-miss in the rest of the square. Or you could use the same colors in every square but change their sequence, using every possible permutation, as in the Mosaic Skirt, page 41.

The traditional way of tying a project together was to always use the same color for the last round of every square and for borders and details. This was usually black. But don't let that prevent you from using your favorite color. A rich blue is used most successfully in the Out-of-the-Blue Jacket (page 13), and even white in the Boleros for Big and Little Girls (page 24).

Generally, clear, sharp brights have been used in granny projects. If your taste runs to a more subtle use of color, try pastels or heather tones. A most handsome granny afghan finished recently was done in heather tones of pearl gray, beige, brown and soft blue. It wasn't the least bit funereal and lent a warm note to a starkly modern room setting.

Using a set color combination in a project is a more modern way of working grannies, and the results can be lovely. See the Boleros for Big and Little Girls (page 24), for example. And who says grannies can't be *all* one color? If you love working grannies but prefer a single shade, see how well it looks in the afghan on page 78.

In many of the following projects the colors used in the sample are specified. Feel free to substitute, change, add or subtract colors as you like. It's your project and it should reflect your likes and dislikes, your good taste and your own creative spirit.

MAKING LARGE PIECES FROM SMALL GRANNIES

Nothing is so sad as a pile of granny squares lying neglected in a box at the back of a closet shelf. You can make the squares on the run, but you have to settle down to assemble a project. A plan of attack will convert the job from a dull chore to a creative experience.

The most common way to work with the granny square is to join square modules of equal size (see Drawing 1) or to join granny variations—units made in triangles, pentagons, hexagons or octagons (see Drawing 2). A simple building-block technique is used.

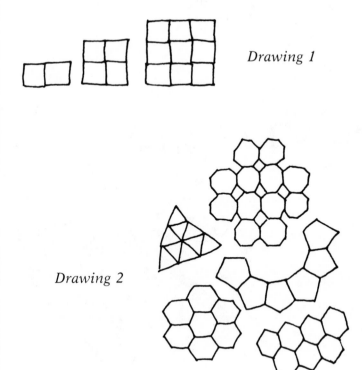

Drawing 1

Drawing 2

There are other exciting ways to build a large piece from the individual granny squares. One is to combine units of different sizes and shapes in one design (see Drawing 3). Another is to combine granny squares with solid crochet in strips or shaped sections (see Drawing 4). The latter technique was used for such items as the Out-of-the-Blue Jacket and the Out-of-the-Ordinary Crib Afghan (pages 13 and 87).

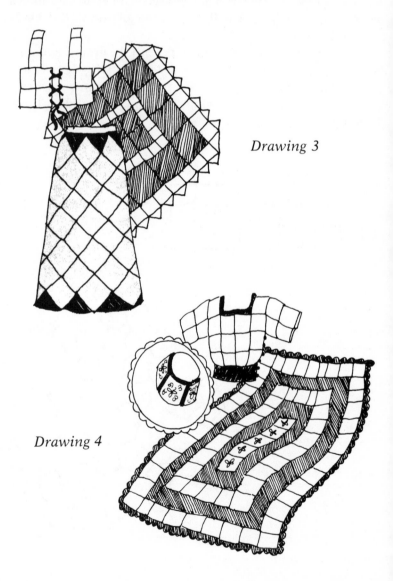

Drawing 3

Drawing 4

JOINING GRANNY SQUARES

You can sew grannies together using a blunt yarn needle or you can crochet them together.

One way to sew grannies is to butt the edges together and weave the yarn back and forth from edge to edge (see Drawing 1). A second method is to butt the edges and use a whipstitch for the joining (see Drawing 2).

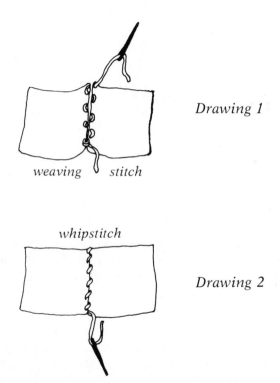

weaving   stitch

Drawing 1

whipstitch

Drawing 2

These techniques are almost invisible if done on the wrong side with matching yarn. But you can achieve an interesting effect by using yarn in a color that contrasts with the squares.

To crochet the squares together, use a slip stitch or single crochet (see Drawing 3). If you work the latter on the right side, you'll end up with a handsome ridged effect. Here, too, you can use yarn in a contrasting color for the joining or use one of the joinings illustrated in the following directions. Clearly, some of these joinings can also be used to add a little width or length to the over-all size of an article.

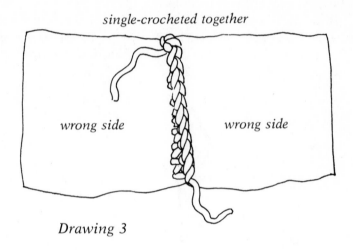

single-crocheted together

wrong side   wrong side

Drawing 3

JOINING A

1st row With right side facing, sl st in a corner of square, ch 3, dc in each st across edge to next corner; ch 3, turn. **2nd row (wrong side)** Skip first dc, work dc around post of next dc (ridge formed on right side), work dc around post of each dc and ch at beg of first row. Break off. Work across edge of adjoining square in same manner.

Hold squares with wrong sides facing and joining edges matching. Work row of sc through matching dc across edge (ridge formed). Break off.

JOINING B

1st row Sl st in corner of a square, ch 3, dc in each st across to next corner. Break off. Work across adjoining square in same manner.

Hold squares right sides facing and joining edges matching. With yarn and tapestry needle, whipstitch pieces tog, working through 1 lp only—outer lp—of each st (2 small ridges formed by unworked lps on right side). Break off.

JOINING A

JOINING B

JOINING C

Dc across 1 edge of each of 2 squares as for joining B.

Hold squares wrong sides facing and joining edges matching. Crochet row of sl st through matching dc, working through 1 lp only— inner lp—of each st (heavy ridge formed by sl sts and 2 light ridges, one on each side of sl sts, formed by unworked lps). Break off.

JOINING D

1st row Sl st in corner of a square, ch 7, sk 3 sts, dc in next st, * ch 3, sk 3 sts, dc in next st. Repeat from * to next corner; ch 5, turn.

2nd row Sc in center st of first sp, ch 2, dc in next dc, * ch 2, sc in center st of next sp, ch 2, dc in next dc. Repeat from * across, ending with dc in 3rd ch of ch-7; ch 7, turn.

3rd row Sk first dc, dc in next dc, * ch 3, dc in next dc. Repeat from * across, ending with dc in 3rd ch of ch-5; ch 5, turn.

4th row Repeat 2nd row. Omit ch 7. Break off.

Work across side of adjoining square in same manner. Hold squares right sides facing and joining edges matching. With yarn and tapestry needle, sew the first 2 matching dc tog, then sew next 2 matching dc tog, leaving loose strand between stitches. Continue across in this manner. Break off.

JOINING C

JOINING D

TIPS ON FITTING THE GRANNY

When you make granny square clothes designed around the building-block technique, you run up against the problem that the grannies, joined, end up as a large square or rectangle — and the human body is neither. If you're making the sort of garment for which precise sizing and shaping isn't critical, plan it this way: decide on the area that must fit. In a sweater, for example, it might be around the bustline. Divide the measurement by the number of units you would like to cover that area; say the bust measurement is 32" and you would like the sweater 8 units around—4 across the front of the sweater and 4 across the back. Divide 32" by 8 for a module size of 4". If you prefer a sweater to fit loosely, make a slightly larger size unit. If you want a clingy sweater, subtract ½" from 4" and make each granny square 3½" x 3½". Incidentally, that ½" is a pretty reliable stretch allowance for any granny.

CAUTION: Once you decide the size of the module, you're stuck with it, and every other measurement must be a multiple of it. The opening of the sweater can fall only at the edge of a module, so the armhole or neckline edge may fall a little lower or higher than you want it.

The obvious and correct conclusion to draw about these sizing and shaping limitations is that the building-block technique, used alone, does not lend itself to making clothes that curve around the body. You can moderate the limitations by using tapered modules in areas of a garment where you would like an increase in fullness or snugness. To enlarge a module, use a taller stitch (a double crochet is longer than a half double crochet), a larger hook or thicker material on one or more rounds or even sides of the module. To reduce the module, use the shortest stitch, a smaller hook or thinner material on one or more rounds of the module. To produce some tapered modules, try using one hook on half of each round of the module and a smaller size hook on the other half of each round to produce a "square" that looks like Drawing 1. With such tricks at your disposal, you can do a certain amount of fitting, but you still may not be able to size your module exactly. In this case, always crochet the module smaller, for granny modules, like all crocheting, stretch easily.

Drawing 1

Another way to design fitted clothing is to combine grannies with regular crochet and use the regular crochet to achieve the crucial shaping and fit. Look at the startling difference in the shapes of the same items in Drawing 2—one made with and one without the aid of regular crochet. The gussets of

Drawing 2

regular crochet (rows of single or double crochet or rows of shells) give the granny square vest the necessary fullness through the bust without sacrificing the snug fit at the waist. The panels of regular crochet in the skirt permit it to hug the waist and hips but flare out gracefully at the bottom.

When you plan your own design for a fitted outfit, decide where the shaping is critical and plan the regular crochet in that area. For example, if you would like a sweater to stop exactly at your waist and you do not want it loose around the bottom, let the last granny squares stop above the waist and single-crochet a waistband to cover the distance between the lower units and waist. Then ease the granny squares onto the waistband when you sew the units together.

If you want a garment to fit very precisely or have a very specific shape, here's still another way to do it: treat the joined grannies like fabric, as we did in our Diamond Jim Tie (page 69). Pin a dress or coat pattern (or whatever you are making) on the joined granny units. Handling the joined grannies on the sewing machine like knit fabric, run two rows of machine stitching around the outer edge of the pattern to prevent raveling. Next, cut outside the stitching line. Treat the parts like regular pattern pieces, pinning and stitching them together. If the shaped section is located along an outer edge of the garment—the neckline, perhaps—finish the edge with single- or double-crochet stitches worked over the line of machine stitching and the new edge.

TIPS FOR MAKING BEAUTIFUL GRANNIES

Buying Yarn If you are making a granny square project of only a few colors, buy all the yarn of a given color at one time and check to see that it's all of the same dye lot. Variations of a shade in adjoining squares may spoil the appearance of your work. (Dye lots are usually numbered; all hanks or balls of yarn of one color should be stamped with the same number.)

Cut Ends Work over the tails of yarn as you go and you will not have the trouble of weaving in those pesky ends later.

Time-Saver If you are making a great many squares all in the same color sequence, make a goodly number (let's say twelve) of first rounds, putting them aside to complete later. Then work the second round on all your squares and so on. Working in this way, with just one color of yarn, will save time — no picking up a new ball at the end of one round. And it may mean that you have to tuck only one ball of yarn in your purse when you carry your crochet with you.

Measuring Amounts When you start a project, it's worth while ripping out your first granny square so that you can measure the yarn consumed in each round. Jot down the yardage required. Then you'll know if you have enough length in your bits and pieces to make a complete round.

Changing Colors You can change colors after each round, every other round, or as you desire. When changing colors, break off yarn after the joining at end of the round has been worked. Then make loop on hook with new color and sl st in the joining st of previous round or in the space specified in the directions. If you do not wish to change colors but the next round starts in a space or stitch a few stitches from where you just ended, don't break off. Just sl st over those intervening sts and into the space or st where the next round should start. Then ch 3 (or whatever the directions call for), and you're all set to go on.

Right Side Always work each round with the right side of work facing you, unless otherwise specified. The right side is the side facing you as you work the first round.

Gauge Some crocheters tend to work more tightly than others. If you find your square is popping up in the middle or cupping, try working a little more loosely. Or you can add an extra ch st between each shell as necessary to keep the square flat.

Beginning Chain Directions usually say "ch 4" or "5" or "6" at the beginning of a square. If you find that the ring that is formed is too small for you to work conveniently into, add an extra chain or two. Conversely, if the beginning ring leaves an unattractive hole in the center of a square, make one or two fewer chains at the beginning.

Working into Corners More stitches are worked into corner spaces than elsewhere in most grannies. If the stitches seem to pile up or are hard to get into the small space, push the first few stitches to the right with your thumbnail to make room for the other stitches. Or add one extra chain stitch when working corners.

Edgings Edgings are the icing on the cake, and you can surround your granny squares with all varieties. Tailored edgings of solid single or double crochet can provide a much-needed calming border to a freewheeling granny square design. Fancy shell ruffles or a picot edging, as in the Out-of-the-Ordinary Crib Afghan on page 87, will contain your project triumphantly.

Laundering If your work has become soiled, wash it by hand before blocking. Launder cotton-thread work in thick suds of a mild soap and hot water; wash woolens in cold-water soap or mild soap and lukewarm water. Squeeze but do not wring the article. Rinse in lukewarm water several times until soap is thoroughly removed. Roll in a bath towel to absorb some of the moisture. Some synthetic yarns are machine washable. Follow manufacturer's directions on the label.

Blocking If you have laundered your work, block it while still damp. Place the article wrong side up on a flat, padded surface. Gently stretch and shape it to the desired measurements; pin to surface, using rustproof pins. Pin corners of grannies first. Press through a dry cloth with a hot iron, being careful not to let the weight of the iron rest on the article. Let dry thoroughly before unpinning or the work may pull out of shape.

If you have not had to launder your work, pin the dry article on a padded surface; press through a damp cloth or with a steam iron.

Block all matching squares together so they will be the

same size. If there are too many, block one and draw a pattern of it. Then block all others to the pattern. When squares of different sizes have to match, such as the small ones in the Rugged Hearth Rug that fit around the 3 large ones (page 93), block the large squares first, then block the small ones to fit. Sometimes they have to be stretched or held in a bit. After joining, you can give your creations one final light steaming on the wrong side.

Lining When you want to line a project, block the granny squares and join them together to form the main basic shapes. Then lay the pieces on your lining material and trace around them in chalk, or pin an outline of the shape onto the material. Allow ½" seam allowance when you cut. Follow the same procedure for constructing the lining as you do for putting the crochet work together, making a seam where you would use a joining stitch for the crochet. Attach the lining to the crochet project, wrong sides facing.

Suggested fabrics: cotton, cotton jersey, silk or washable, shrinkproof dye-fast synthetics.

BEING CREATIVE WITH GRANNIES

Half the fun of working grannies is in creating your own projects, developing your own ideas. If you can visualize a bikini in squares, there's no reason why you can't have a granny square bikini. Here are a few variations on the granny which will give you the basic building blocks of hundreds of new projects. To spark your own creative instincts, a list of possible uses for grannies is found on page 157.

GOLD AND PINK SQUARE

Size Square measures approximately 8½" when worked with knitting worsted and aluminum crochet hook size **F**.

Starting at center, with gold ch 6. Join with sl st to form ring.

1st rnd Ch 5, dc in ring, (ch 2, dc in ring) 6 times; ch 2; join with sl st in 2nd ch of ch-5.

2nd rnd Sl st in next ch-2 sp, ch 3, y o hook, draw up lp in same sp, y o, draw through 2 lps on hook, (2 lps remain on hook), y o, draw up lp in same sp, y o, draw through 2 lps on hook, y o, draw through remaining 3 lps on hook (2-dc cl made), * ch 4, y o, draw up lp in next sp, y o, draw through 2 lps on hook, y o, draw up lp in same sp, y o, draw through 2 lps on hook, y o, draw up lp in same sp, y o, draw through 3 lps on hook, y o, draw through remaining 3 lps on hook, (3-dc cl completed). Repeat from * 6 times more; ch 4; join with sl st to top of ch-3. Break off.

3rd rnd With pink sc in any ch-4 sp, * ch 4, 2 sc in same sp, ch 4, sc in same sp, ch 4, sc in next sp. Repeat from * 6 times more; ch 4, 2 sc in same sp, ch 4, sc in same sp, ch 2; dc in first sc.

4th rnd * Ch 4, sc in next ch-4 sp. Repeat from * around, ending with ch 2, dc in last dc of preceding rnd.

5th rnd Repeat 4th rnd.

6th rnd * Ch 8, sk next sp, sc in next sp (ch 4, sc in next sp) 4 times. Repeat from * 3 times more, ending last repeat with 3 ch-4 lps, ch 2, dc in last dc of preceding rnd.

7th rnd * Ch 5, work 14 sc in next ch-8 lp, (ch 5, sc in next sp) 4 times. Repeat from * 3 times more, ending last repeat with 3 ch-5 lps, ch 2, dc in last dc of preceding rnd.

8th rnd * Ch 9, sk next ch-5 lp and next 6 sc, sc in next sc, ch 9, sc in next sc, ch 9, sk next 6 sc and next ch-5 lp, sc in next lp, (ch 5, sc in next lp) twice. Repeat from * 3 times more, ending last repeat with 1 ch-5 lp, ch 3, dc in last dc of preceding rnd.

9th rnd * Ch 5, work 4 sc in next ch-9 lp, for picot ch 4, sc in first ch of ch-4 (picot made), work 4 sc in same lp, in next ch-9 lp work 3 sc, picot, 1 sc, picot and 3 sc, in next lp work 4 sc, picot and 4 sc, (ch 5, 2 sc in next ch-5 lp) twice. Repeat from * 3 times more, ending last repeat with 1 ch-5 lp, ch 3, dc in last dc of preceding rnd. Break off.

OLIVE AND BLUE SQUARE

Size Square measures approximately 3″ when worked with knitting worsted and aluminum crochet hook size G.

Starting at center with olive, ch 4. Join with sl st to form ring.

1st rnd Ch 3, work 11 dc in ring (12 dc, counting ch-3 as 1 dc); join with sl st to top of ch-3. Break off.

2nd rnd Attach blue with sc in last dc made, * ch 6, sk next 2 dc, sc in next dc. Repeat from * 3 times more, ending last repeat with sl st in first sc.

3rd rnd Sl st in first ch-6 lp, ch 3, work 3 dc in same lp; to make picot ch 4, sc in 4th ch from hook (picot completed), work 4 more dc in same lp, * work picot, in next ch-6 lp work 4 dc, picot and 4 dc. Repeat from * twice more; work picot; join with sl st to top of ch-3. Break off.

MAUVE, RUST AND LAVENDER SQUARE

Size Square measures approximately 8½″ when worked with knitting worsted and aluminum crochet hook size F.

Starting at center with mauve, ch 4. Join with sl st to form ring.

1st rnd Ch 3, work 3 dc in ring, (ch 3, 4 dc in ring) 3 times; ch 3; join with sl st to top of ch-3. Break off.

2nd rnd With rust sc in any ch-3 sp, (ch 10, sc in next ch-3 sp) 3 times; ch 10, sl st in first sc.

3rd rnd (Work 12 sc in next ch-10 lp, sc in next sc) 3 times; 12 sc in next ch-10 lp.

4th rnd Ch 5, * dec 1 sc as follows: draw up lp in each of next 2 sc, y o hook, draw through all 3 lps on hook (dec completed), sc in each of next 8 sc, dec 1 sc, ch 5, sk next sc between lps. Repeat from * twice more; dec 1 sc, sc in each of next 8 sc, dec 1 sc.

5th rnd * Ch 5, 4 dc in next ch-5 lp, ch 5, dec 1 sc in next 2 sc, sc in each of next 6 sc, dec 1 sc. Repeat from * 3 times more.

6th rnd * (Ch 5, 4 dc in next ch-5 lp) twice; ch 5, dec 1 sc in next 2 sc, sc in each of next 4 sc, dec 1 sc. Repeat from * 3 times more.

7th rnd * Ch 5, 4 dc in next ch-5 lp, ch 5, work sc, ch 1 and sc in next ch-5 lp, ch 5, 4 dc in next ch-5 lp, ch 5, dec 1 sc in next 2 sc, sc in next 2 sc, dec 1 sc. Repeat from * 3 times more.

8th rnd Sl st in first lp, ch 3, 3 dc in same lp, * ch 5, sc in next ch-5 lp, ch 5, work sc, ch 5 (corner lp) and sc in next ch-1 sp, ch 5, sc in next ch-5 lp, ch 5, 4 dc in each of next 2 lps. Repeat from * 3 times more, omitting last 4 dc; join with sl st to top of ch-3. Break off.

9th rnd With lavender sl st in any corner ch-5 lp, ch 3, work 3 dc, ch 3 and 4 dc in same lp (first corner) , * (ch 5, sc in next ch-5 lp) twice; ch 5, sc in sp between two 4-dc groups, (ch 5, sc in next ch-5 lp) twice; ch 5, work 4 dc, ch 3 and 4 dc in next corner ch-5 lp (another corner). Repeat from * twice more; (ch 5, sc in next ch-5 lp) twice; ch 5, sc in sp between 2 groups, (ch 5, sc in next ch-5 lp) twice; ch 5; join.

10th rnd Sl st in each st to corner ch-3 sp, sl st in corner sp, work first corner in same sp, *(ch 5, sc in next ch-5 lp) 6 times; ch 5, work corner in next sp. Repeat from * twice more; (ch 5, sc in next ch-5 lp) 6 times; ch 5; join. Break off.

ORANGE, GOLD AND BROWN SQUARE

Size Square measures approximately 4″ when worked with knitting worsted and aluminum crochet hook size G.

Starting at center with orange, ch 4. Join with sl st to form ring.

1st rnd Ch 3, work 2 dc in ring, (ch 1, 3-dc shell in ring) 3 times; ch 1; join with sl st to top of ch-3. Break off.

2nd rnd With gold sl st in any ch-1 sp, ch 3, in same sp work 2 dc, ch 1 and 3 dc (first corner) * ch 1, in next ch-1 sp work 3 dc, ch 1 and 3 dc (another corner). Repeat from * twice more; ch 1; join. Break off.

3rd rnd With brown sl st in any ch-1 corner sp, ch 6, work dc in same sp (first corner lp), * ch 3, work dc in next ch-1 sp, ch 3, work dc, ch 3 and dc in next ch-1 corner sp (another corner lp). Repeat from * twice more; ch 3, dc in next ch-1 sp, ch 3; join with sl st in 3rd ch of ch-6.

4th rnd Sl st in next ch-3 corner lp, ch 3, work 2 dc, ch 1, and 3 dc in same lp (first corner), * (ch 1, work 3 dc in next ch-3 sp) twice; ch 1, work 3 dc, ch 1 and 3 dc in next corner lp (another corner). Repeat from * twice more; (ch 1, 3 dc in next ch-3 sp) twice; ch 1; join. Break off.

GREEN AND LAVENDER SQUARE

Size Square measures approximately 6″ when worked with knitting worsted and aluminum crochet hook size G.

Starting at center with green, ch 4. Join with sl st to form ring.

1st rnd Work 8 sc in ring; join with sl st to first sc. Break off.

2nd rnd Sl st in first sc, ch 3, work dc in same place as sl st, ch 2, * y o hook, draw up lp in next sc, y o, draw through 2 lps on hook (2 lps remain on hook), y o, draw up lp in same st, y o, draw through 2 lps on hook, y o, draw through remaining 3 lps on hook (2-dc cl made), ch 2. Repeat from * 6 times more; join with sl st to top of ch-3 (eight 2-dc cl made, counting ch-3 as 1 dc). Break off.

3rd rnd With lavender sl st in any ch-2 sp, ch 3, work 2-dc cl in same sp, ch 3, y o, draw up lp in same sp, y o, draw through 2 lps on hook, y o, draw up lp in same sp, y o, draw through 2 lps on hook, y o, draw up lp in same sp, y o, draw through 3 lps on hook, y o, draw through remaining 3 lps on hook (3-dc cl completed—first corner made), * ch 2, work 3-dc cl in next ch-2 sp, ch 2, work 3-dc cl, ch 3 and 3-dc cl in next ch-2 sp (another corner). Repeat from * twice more; ch 2, 3-dc cl in next sp; join. Break off.

4th rnd With green sl st in any corner ch-3 sp, work first corner in same sp, * (ch 2, work 3-dc cl in next ch-2 sp) twice; ch 2, work corner in next ch-2 sp. Repeat from * twice more; (ch 2, work 3-dc cl in next ch-2 sp) twice; ch 2; join. Break off.
5th rnd With lavender sl st in any corner ch-3 sp, work first corner in same sp, * (ch 2, work 3-dc cl in next ch-2 sp) 3 times; ch 2, work corner in next ch-3 sp. Repeat from * twice more; (ch 2, work 3-dc cl in next sp) 3 times; ch 2; join. Break off.

RED AND BLUE SQUARE

Size Square measures approximately 5½″ when worked with knitting worsted and aluminum crochet hook size G.

Starting at center with red, ch 4. Join with sl st to form ring.
1st rnd Work 8 sc in ring; join with sl st to first sc.
2nd rnd Ch 3, work dc in same place as sl st, * ch 2, y o hook, draw up lp in next st, y o, draw through 2 lps on hook (2 lps remain on hook), y o, draw up lp in same st, y o, draw through 2 lps on hook, y o, draw through remaining 3 lps on hook (2-dc cl made). Repeat from * 6 times more ; ch 2; join with sl st to top of ch-3 (16 dc, counting ch-3 as 1 dc). Break off.
3rd rnd With blue sl st in any ch-2 sp, ch 3, work 2 dc, ch 2 and 3 dc in same sp, (first corner), * ch 2, 3-dc shell in next ch-2 sp, ch 2, work 3 dc, ch 2 and 3 dc in next ch-2 sp (another corner). Repeat from * twice more; ch 2, shell in next sp, ch 2; join with sl st to top of ch-3.
4th rnd Sl st in each st to ch-2 corner sp. Work first corner in same sp, * (ch 2, work shell in next ch-2 sp) twice; ch 2, work corner in next corner sp. Repeat from * twice more; (ch 2, shell in next sp) twice; ch 2; join.
5th rnd Sl st in each st to corner ch-2 sp, work first corner in same sp, * (ch 2, shell in next sp) 3 times; ch 2, work corner in next corner sp. Repeat from * twice more; (ch 2, shell in next sp) 3 times; ch 2; join. Break off.

DIFFERENT SHAPES TO CREATE

To fit a garment made of grannies or to fill in the edges of an item such as a shawl, it is sometimes necessary to make grannies in some shape other than the traditional square. Here are a few odd-shaped grannies to help you develop your own designs.

TRIANGLE (One-Quarter of a Traditional Granny Square)

1st row Starting at point A on diagram below, ch 5; in 5th ch from hook work 3 dc, ch 1 and 1 dc. Break off.
2nd row Sl st in first ch-4 lp, ch 4, work 3 dc in same lp, ch 1, in next ch-1 sp work 3 dc, ch 1 and 1 dc. Break off.
3rd row Sl st in first ch-4 lp, ch 4, 3 dc in same lp, ch 1, 3 dc in next ch-1 sp, ch 1, in last sp work 3 dc, ch 1 and 1 dc. Break off.

4th row Sl st in first ch-4 lp, ch 4, 3 dc in same lp, (ch 1, 3 dc in next ch-1 sp) twice; ch 1, in last sp work 3 dc, ch 1 and 1 dc. Break off.
5th row Sl st in first ch-4 lp, ch 4, 3 dc in same lp, * ch 1, 3 dc in next ch-1 sp. Repeat from * to last sp, ch 1, in last sp work 3 dc, ch 1 and 1 dc. Break off.
    Repeat last row for desired size.

TRIANGLE (Half of a Traditional Granny Square)

1st row Starting at center of one edge (point A on diagram, p. 150), ch 5; in 5th ch from hook work 3 dc, ch 1, 3 dc, ch 1 and 1 dc. Break off.
2nd row Sl st in first ch-4 lp, ch 4, work 3 dc in same lp, ch 1, in next ch-1 sp work 3 dc, ch 1 and 3 dc (corner), ch 1, in last sp work 3 dc, ch 1 and 1 dc. Break off.
3rd row Sl st in first ch-4 lp, ch 4, 3 dc in same lp, ch 1, 3 dc in next ch-1 sp, ch 1, corner in next ch-1 corner sp, ch 1, 3 dc in next sp, ch 1, in last sp work 3 dc, ch 1 and 1 dc. Break off.

4th row Sl st in first ch-4 lp, ch 4, 3 dc in same lp, (ch 1, 3 dc in next ch-1 sp) twice; ch 1, corner in ch-1 corner sp, (ch 1, 3 dc in next sp) twice; ch 1, in last sp work 3 dc, ch 1 and 1 dc. Break off.

5th row Work sl st in first ch-4 lp, ch 4, 3 dc in same lp, * ch 1, 3 dc in next sp. Repeat from * to corner, ch 1, work corner in corner sp, ** ch 1, 3 dc in next sp. Repeat from ** to last sp, in last sp work 3 dc, ch 1 and 1 dc. Break off.

Repeat last row for desired size.

RECTANGLE

Size Rectangle measures approximately 3¾" x 5¾" when worked with knitting worsted and aluminum crochet hook size G.

Starting at center, ch 6. Join with sl st to form ring.
1st rnd Ch 3, 2 dc in ring, ch 1, 3 sc in ring, ch 1, 3 dc in ring, ch 1, 3 sc in ring, ch 1; join with sl st to top of ch-3. Break off.
2nd rnd Sl st in first ch-1 sp made on last rnd, ch 4, work dc, h dc and sc in same sp (first corner made), ch 1, in next sp work sc,

h dc, dc, ch 1 and dc (2nd corner), ch 1, in next sp work dc, ch 1, dc, h dc and sc (3rd corner), ch 1, in next sp work a 2nd corner, ch 1; join with sl st to 3rd ch of ch-4. Break off.

3rd rnd Work first corner as for last rnd, ch 1, 3 sc in next ch-1 sp, ch 1, work 2nd corner in next ch-1 corner sp, ch 1, 2 dc in next sp, ch 1, work 3rd corner in next corner sp, ch 1, 3 sc in next sp, ch 1, work a 2nd corner in next corner sp, ch 1, 2 dc in next sp, ch 1; join. Break off.

4th rnd Work first corner as for 2nd rnd, (ch 1, 3 sc in next ch-1 sp) twice; ch 1, work 2nd corner in next ch-1 corner sp, (ch 1, 2 dc in next sp) twice; ch 1, work 3rd corner in next corner sp, (ch 1, 3 sc in next sp) twice; ch 1, work a 2nd corner in next corner sp, (ch 1, 2 dc in next sp) twice; ch 1; join. Break off.

5th rnd Sl st in first ch-1 sp made on last rnd, ch 4, work 3 dc in same sp (first corner) , * ch 1, 3 dc in next ch-1 sp *. Repeat from * to * to next ch-1 corner sp, ch 1, work 3 dc, ch 1 and 1 dc in corner sp (2nd corner), ** ch 1, 2 dc in next sp **. Repeat from * * to ** to next corner sp, ch 1, work dc, ch 1 and 3 dc in corner sp. Repeat from * to * to next corner sp, ch 1, work a

2nd corner in corner sp, ch 1. Repeat from ** to ** to end, ch 1; join. Break off.

Repeat last rnd for desired size.

PENTAGON

Size Pentagon measures approximately 6″ across when worked with knitting worsted and aluminum crochet hook size G.

Starting at center, ch 4. Join with sl st to form ring.

1st rnd Ch 3, work 1 dc in ring, (ch 1, 2 dc in ring) 4 times; ch 1; join with sl st to top of ch-3. Break off.

2nd rnd Sl st in any ch-1 sp, ch 3, in same sp work 1 dc, ch 1 and 2 dc (first corner), * ch 1, in next ch-1 sp work 2 dc, ch 1 and 2 dc (another corner). Repeat from * 3 times more (5 corners); ch 1; join. Break off.

3rd rnd Sl st in any ch-1 corner sp, work first corner in same sp, * ch 1, 2-dc shell in next ch-1 sp, ch 1, corner in next corner sp. Repeat from * 3 times more; ch 1, shell in next sp, ch 1; join. Break off.

4th rnd Sl st in any ch-1 corner sp, work first corner in same sp, * (ch 1, shell in next ch-1 sp) twice; ch 1, corner in next corner sp. Repeat from * 3 times more; (ch 1, shell in next sp) twice; ch 1; join. Break off.

5th rnd Sl st in any ch-1 corner sp, work first corner in same sp, * ch 1, shell in next ch-1 sp *. Repeat from * to * to next corner, ch 1, corner in corner sp. Continue around in pattern, ch 1; join. Break off.

Repeat last rnd for desired size.

HEXAGON

Size Hexagon measures approximately 7″ from a corner to opposite corner when worked with knitting worsted and aluminum crochet hook size G.

Starting at center, ch 6. Join with sl st to form ring.

1st rnd Ch 3, dc in ring, (ch 1, 2 dc in ring) 5 times; ch 1; join with sl st to top of ch-3. Break off.

2nd rnd Sl st in any ch-1 sp, ch 3, in same sp work dc, ch 1 and 2 dc (first corner), * ch 1, in next sp work 2 dc, ch 1 and 2 dc (another corner). Repeat from * 4 times more; ch 1; join. Break off.

3rd rnd Sl st in any ch-1 corner sp, work first corner in same sp, * ch 1, 2-dc shell in next ch-1 sp, ch 1, corner in next corner sp. Repeat from * 4 times more (6 corners); ch 1, shell in next sp, ch 1; join. Break off.

4th rnd Sl st in any ch-1 corner sp, work first corner in same sp, * (ch 1, shell in next ch-1 sp) twice; ch 1, corner in next corner sp. Repeat from * 4 times more; (ch 1, shell in next sp) twice; ch 1; join. Break off.

5th rnd Sl st in any ch-1 corner sp, work first corner in same sp, * ch 1, shell in next ch-1 sp *. Repeat from * to * to next corner, ch 1, corner in corner sp. Repeat from * to * to next corner, ch 1, corner in corner sp. Continue around in pattern, ch 1; join. Break off.

Repeat last rnd for desired size.

OCTAGON

Size Octagon measures approximately 6¼" when worked with knitting worsted and aluminum crochet hook size G.

Starting at center, ch 6. Join with sl st to form ring.

1st rnd Ch 3, work 2 dc in ring, (ch 1, 3 dc in ring) 3 times; ch 1; join with sl st to top of ch-3. Break off.

2nd rnd Sl st in any ch-1 sp, ch 3, in same sp work 2 dc, ch 1 and 3 dc (first corner), * ch 1, in next ch-1 sp work 3 dc, ch 1 and 3 dc (another corner). Repeat from * twice more (4 corners); ch 1; join with sl st to top of ch-3. Break off.

3rd rnd Sl st in any ch-1 sp, ch 3, in same sp work dc, ch 1 and 2 dc for first corner, (ch 1, in next ch-1 sp work 2 dc, ch 1 and 2 dc for another corner) 7 times (8 corners); ch 1; join. Break off.

4th rnd Sl st in any ch-1 corner sp, in same sp work first corner as for 3rd rnd, * ch 1, 2-dc shell in next ch-1 sp, ch 1, corner as for 3rd rnd in next corner sp. Repeat from * 6 times more; ch 1, shell in next sp, ch 1; join. Break off.

5th rnd Sl st in any ch-1 corner sp, work first corner as for 3rd rnd in same sp, * ch 1, shell in next ch-1 sp *. Repeat from * to * to next corner, ch 1, work corner as for 3rd rnd in corner sp. Continue around in pattern, ch 1; join. Break off.

Repeat last rnd for desired size.

50 IDEAS FOR USING GRANNY SQUARES

Album cover
Appliance covers for toaster,
    blender, mixer, etc.
    (in cotton)
Baby bib
Baby blocks
Baby bunting
Bathmat
Bed jacket
Bed socks
Birdcage cover
Bookmark (tiny squares
    of lightweight
    thread)
Cafe curtains (in lightweight
    cotton)
Car-seat slipcovers
Cat mat
Christmas-tree ornaments
Christmas-tree skirt
Coasters
Covered brick doorstop
Dog bed
Doll clothes
Glass cozies
Golf-club covers
Hatband
Headband
Head scarf
Insertions of
    various grannies in
    plain-color curtains

Lampshade (in fine thread
    with large hook)
Laprobe
Laundry bag
Lingerie cases
Lounge slippers
Man's one-color sleeveless
    sweater
Mirror frame
Mittens
Patches on blue jeans
Room divider
Shawl
Shoe bags for travel
Stole
Tablecloth
Tea cozy
Telephone-book cover
Tennis-racket cover
Turtleneck dickey
Upholstery for bar stools (in
    firm cotton)
Upholstery for breakfast-room
    seats (in firm cotton)
Upholstery for footstool (in
    firm cotton)
Upholstery for patio furni-
    ture (in firm cotton)
Valances
Wall hanging
Washcloth (worked very
    loosely in cotton)